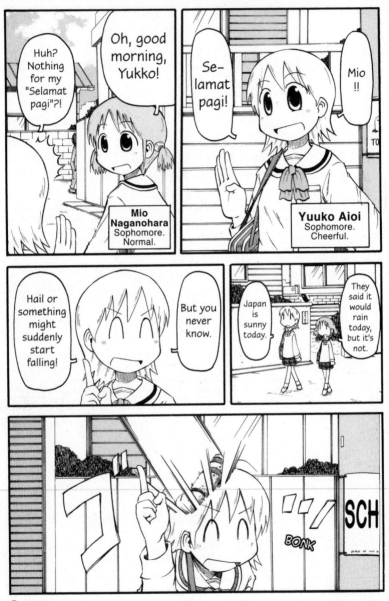

5

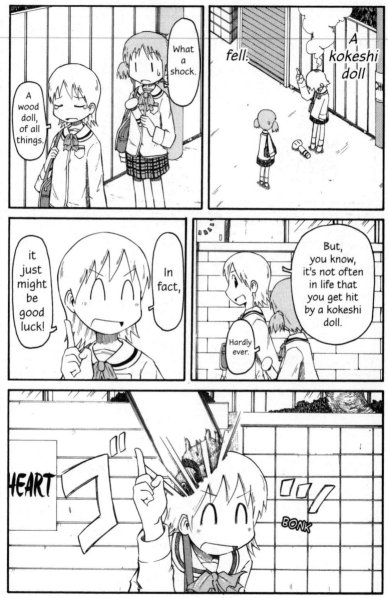

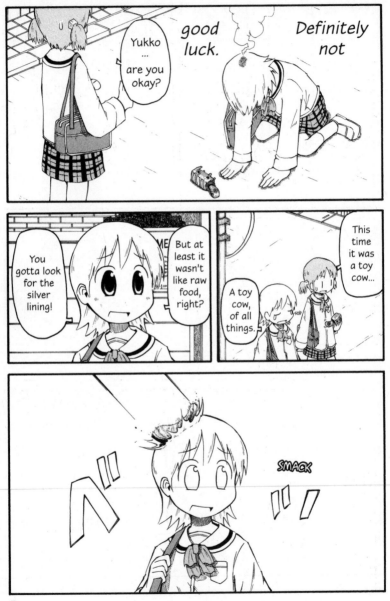

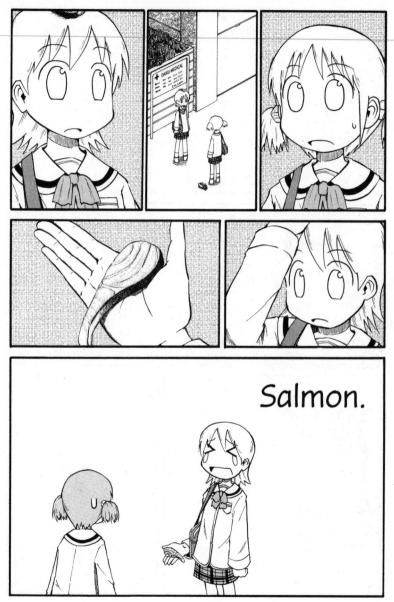

Salmon.

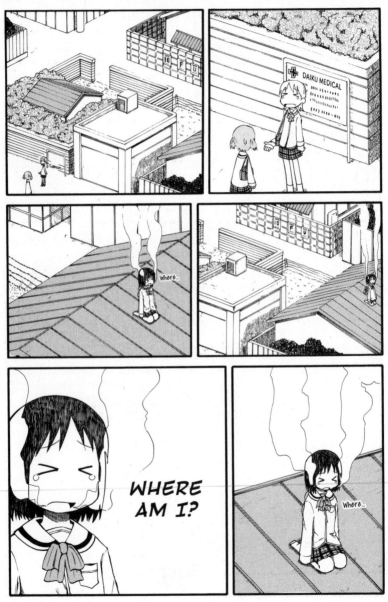

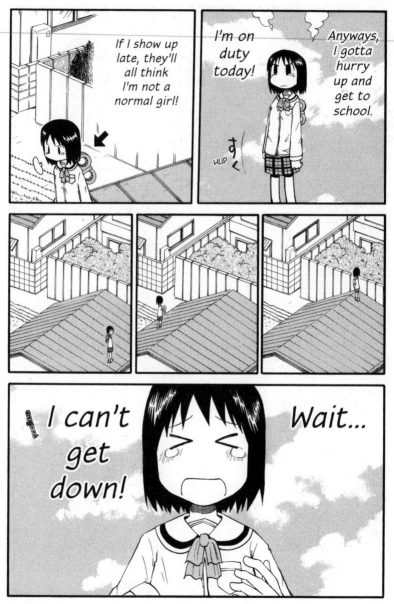

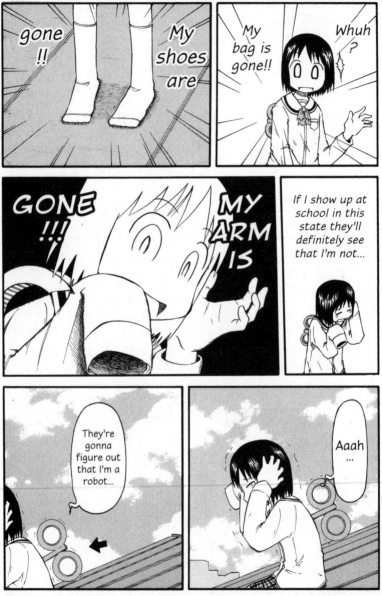

11

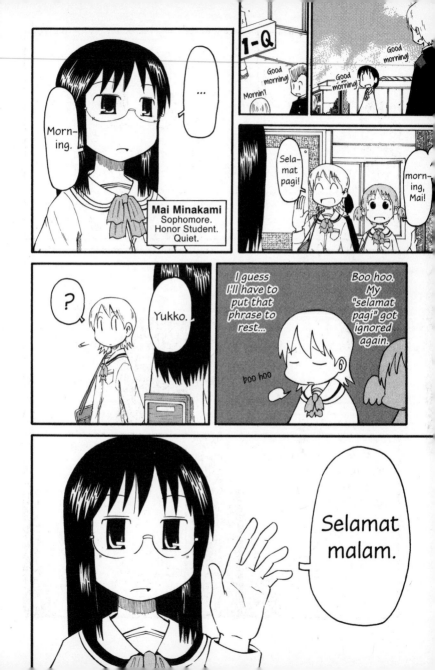

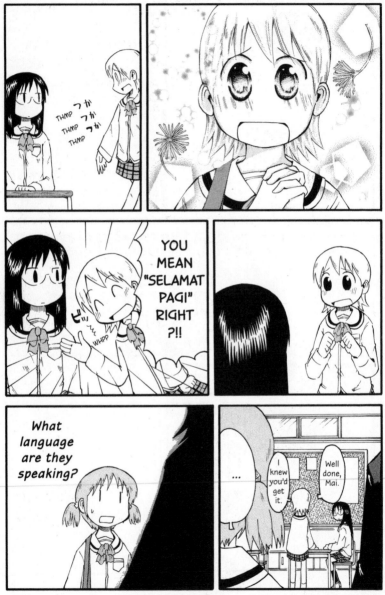

13

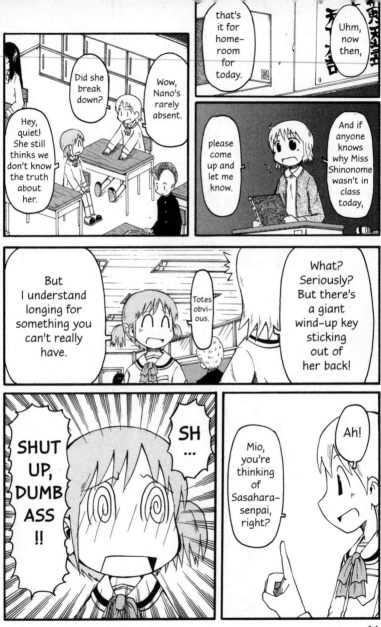

14

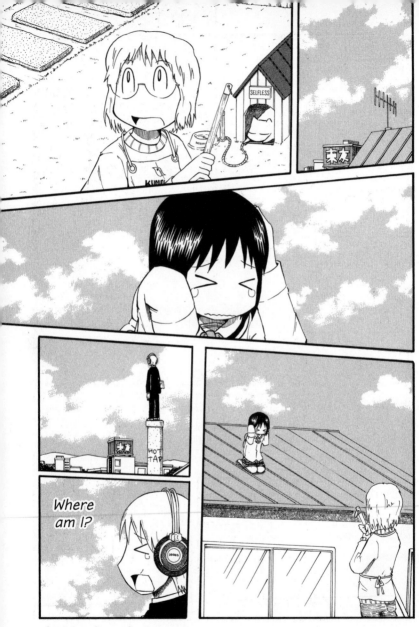

chapter 1: end

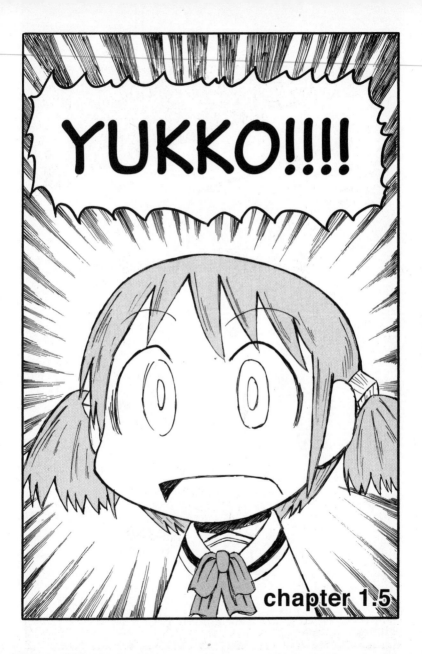

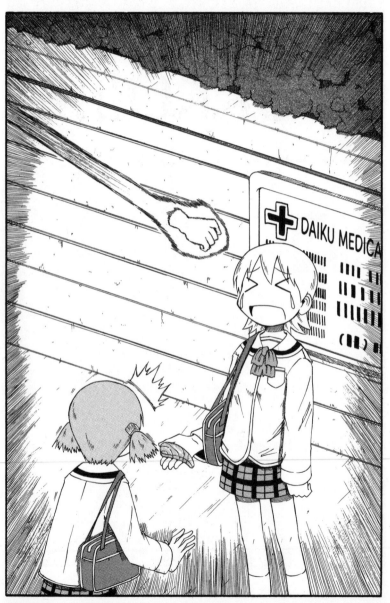

chapter 1.5: end

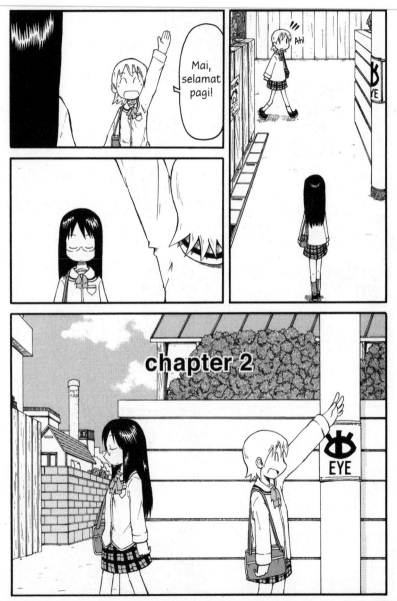

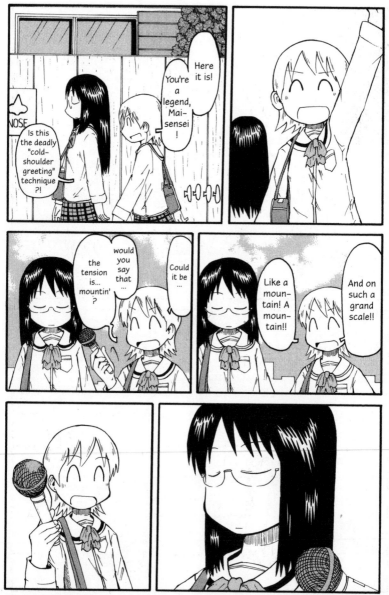

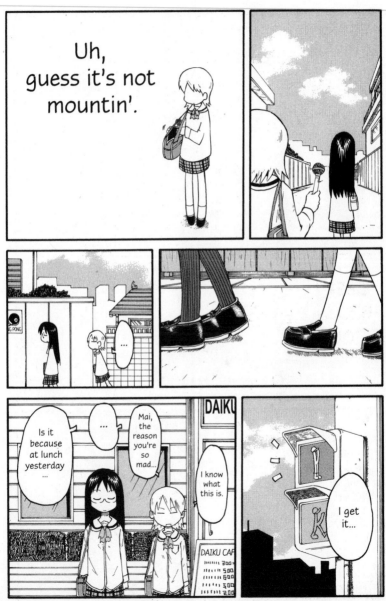

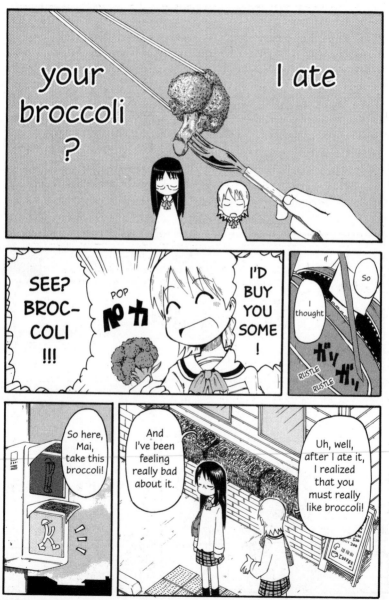

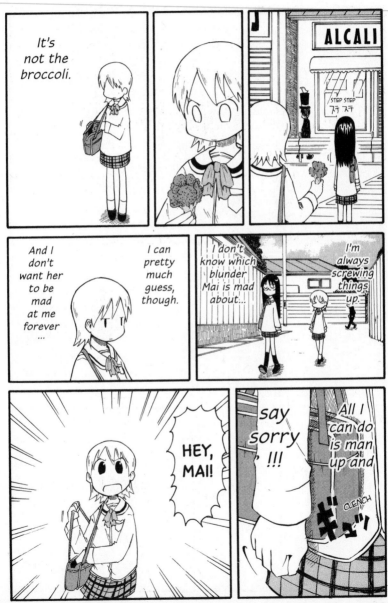

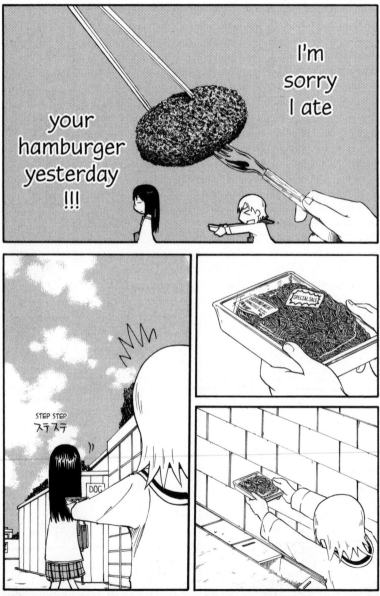

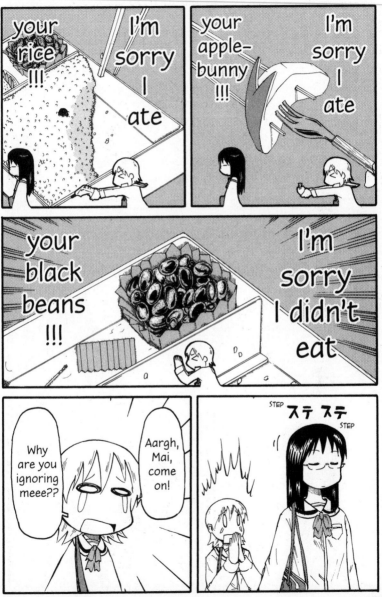

24

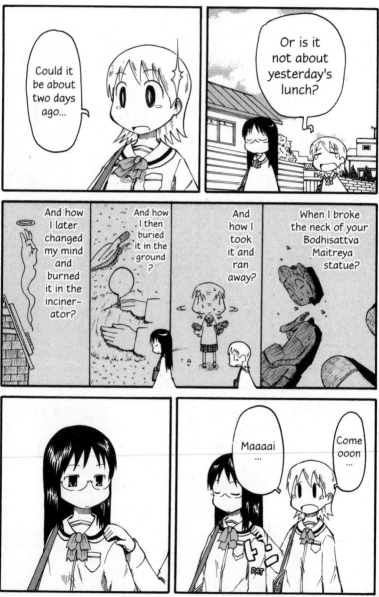

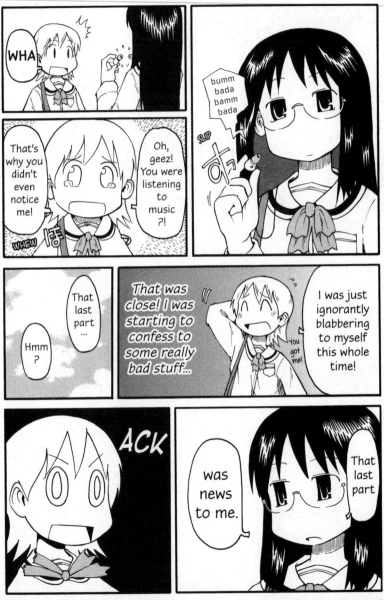

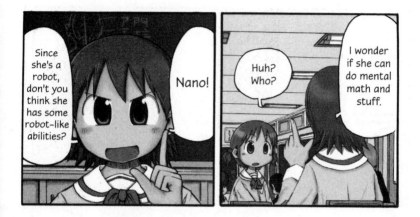

chapter 3

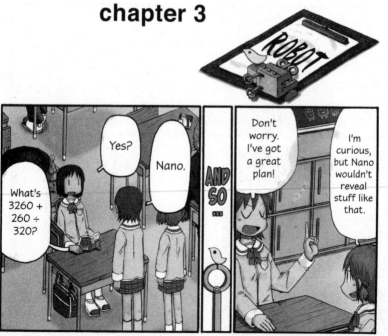

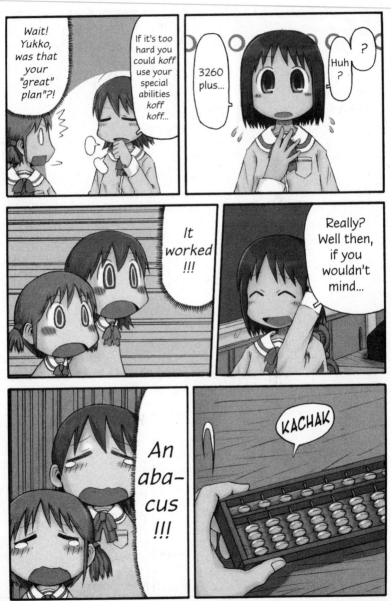

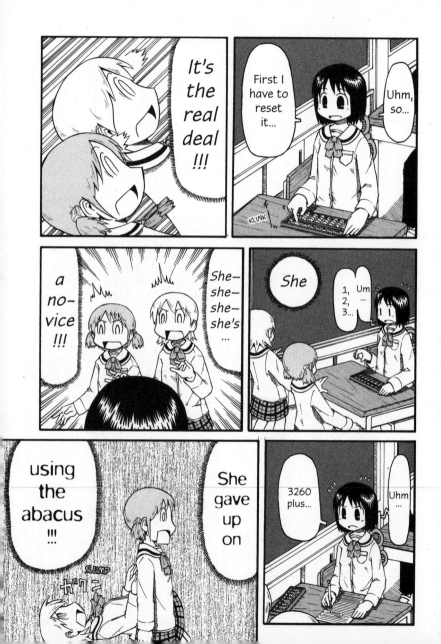

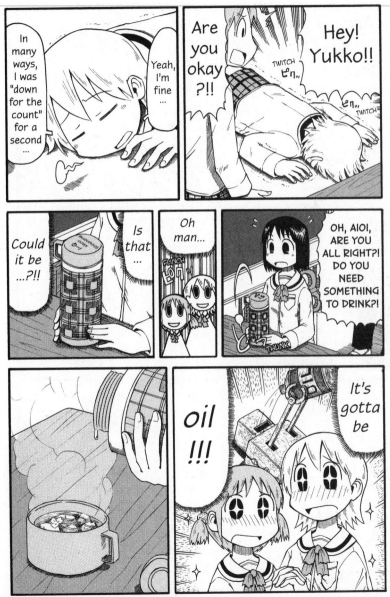

30

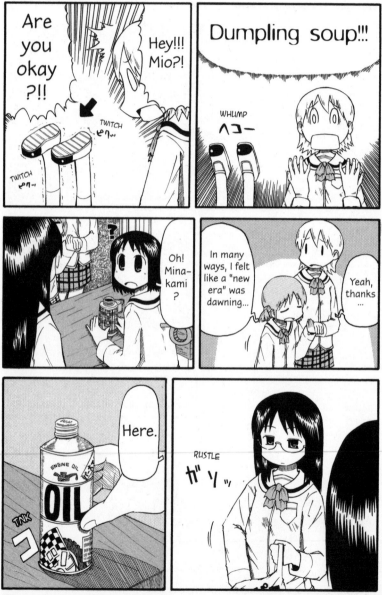

31

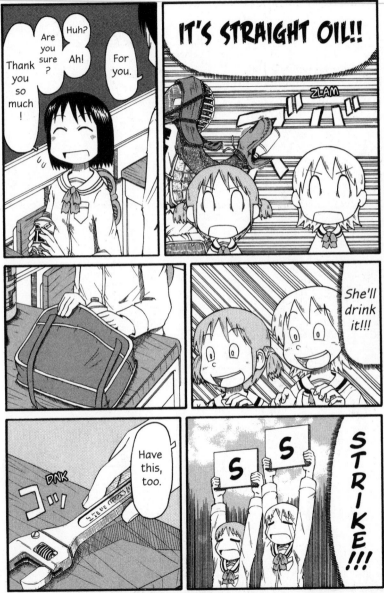

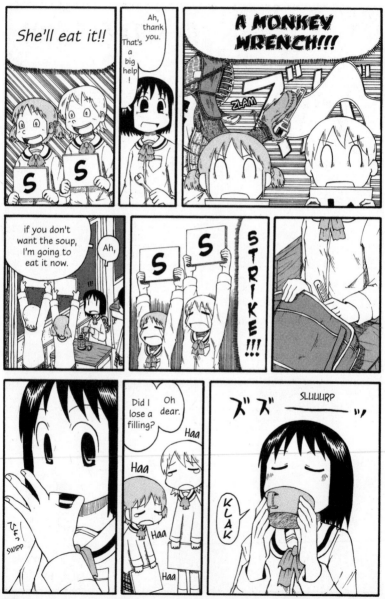

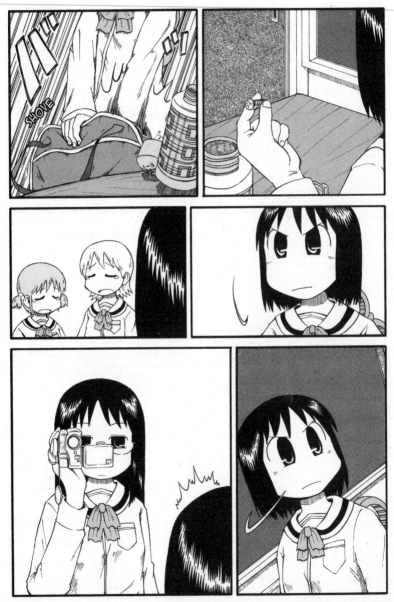

chapter 3: end

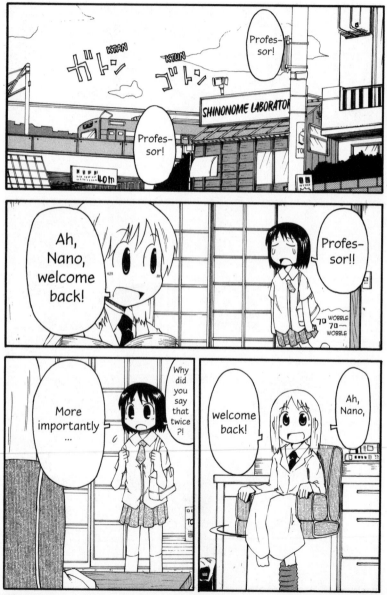

35

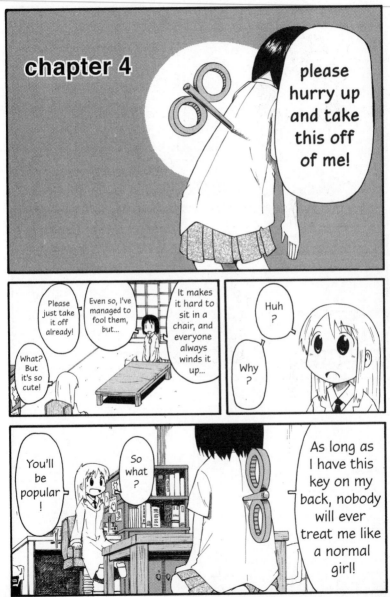

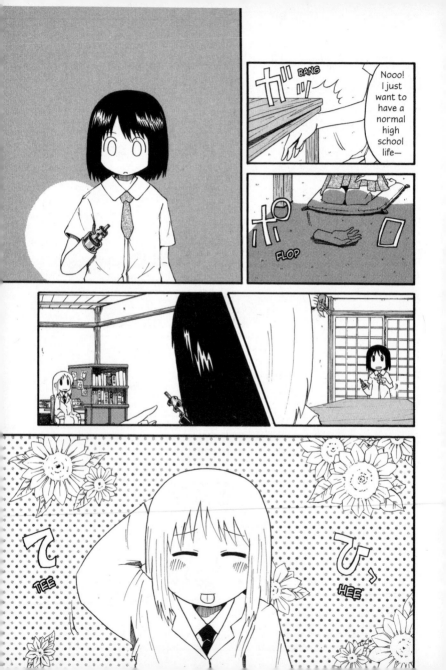

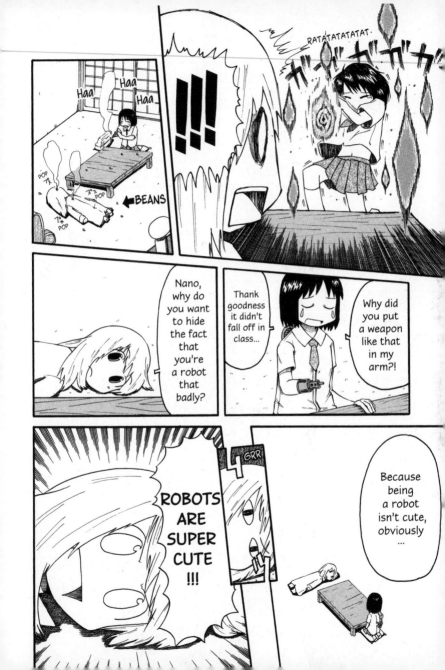

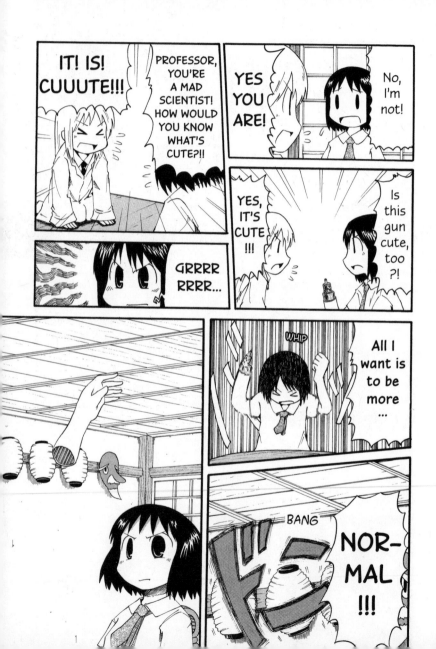

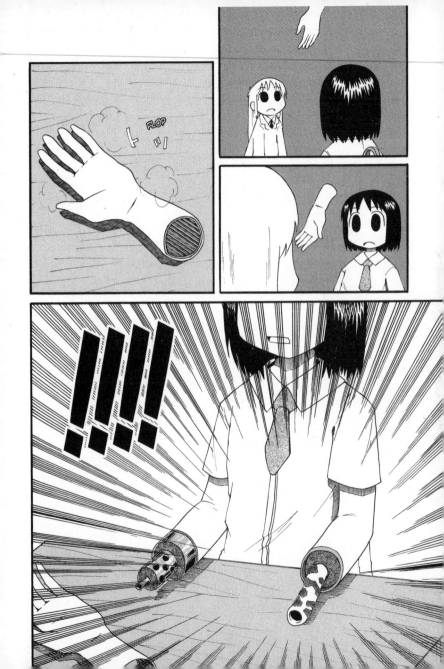

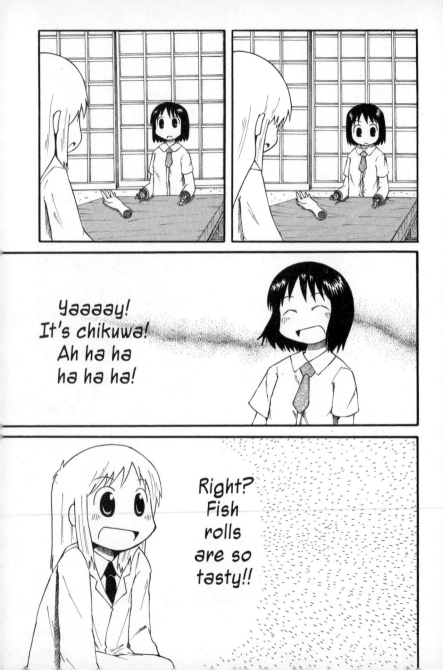

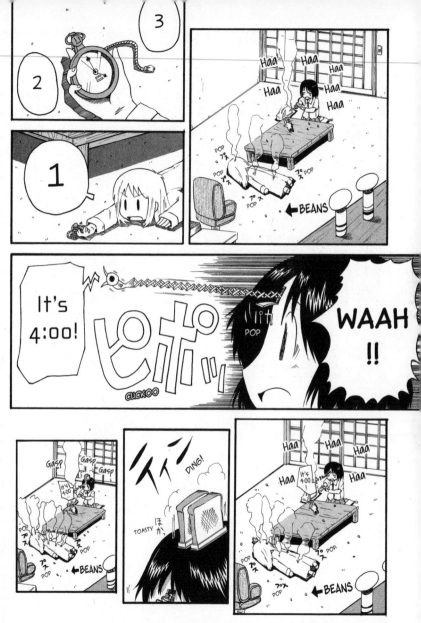

chapter 4: end

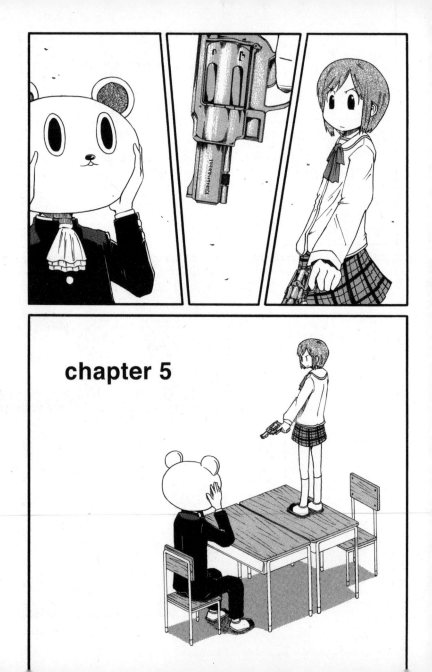

chapter 5

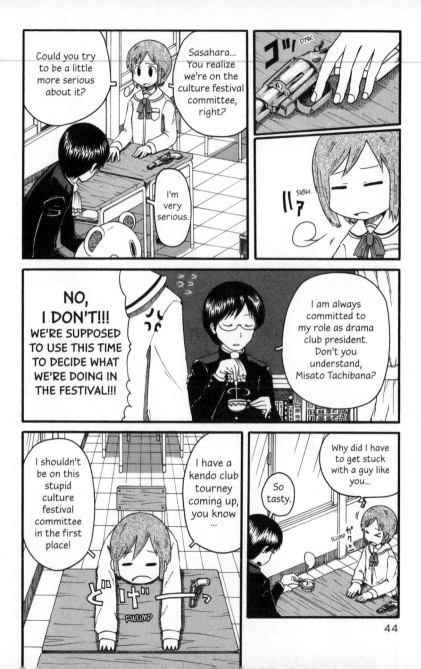

44

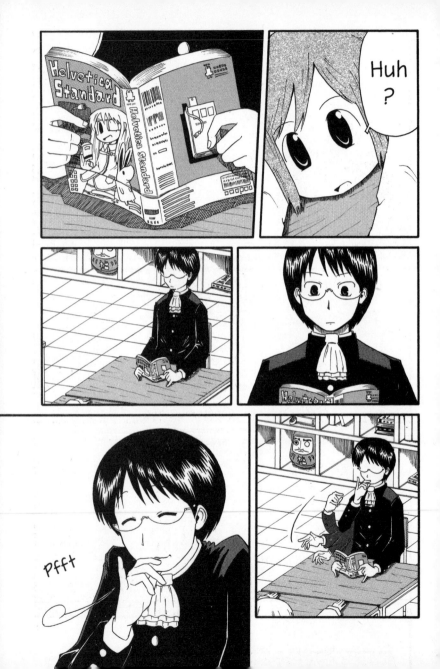

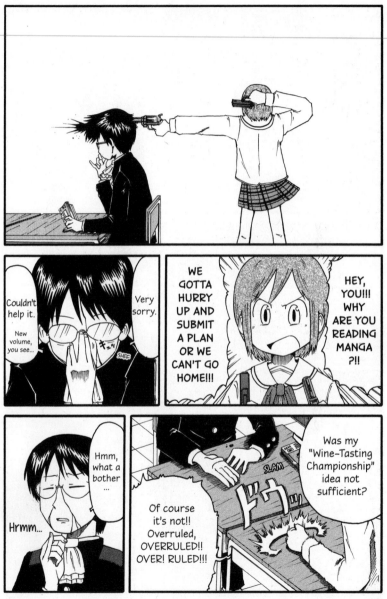

46

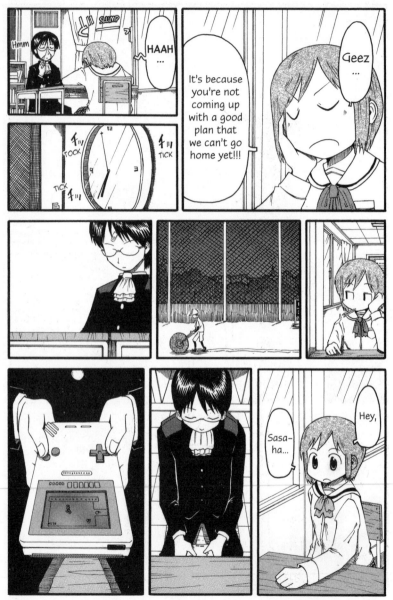

47

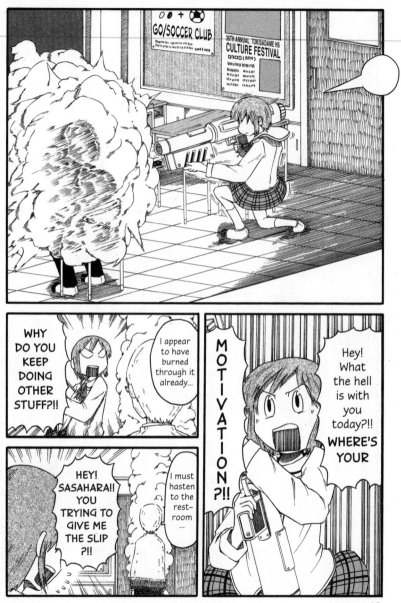

48

she herself hasn't given any suggestions.

More-over, from the start,

As far as I'm concerned, a wine-tasting championship would be just fine.

Misato Tachibana keeps saying no. She seems to be in a poor mood today.

SHUFFLE

SHUFFLE

Thus, if I wish to retire, I have no choice but to present more ideas.

CHK

However, if I were to point that out, my life would surely be forfeit.

Well then, let me give it serious contemplation...

SLIDE

Hmm...

COCONUT MILK

COCONUT MILK

PEACH

INK

Must I then lower myself to think on the level of a commoner?

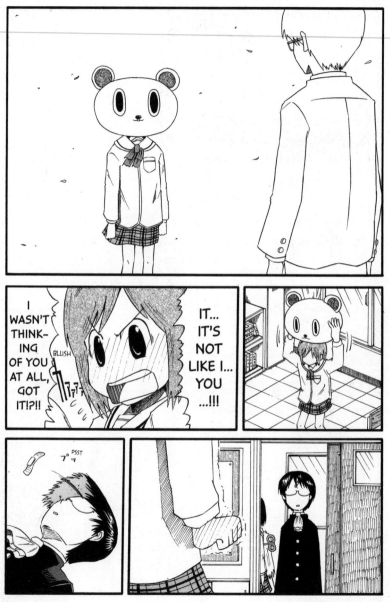

chapter 5: end

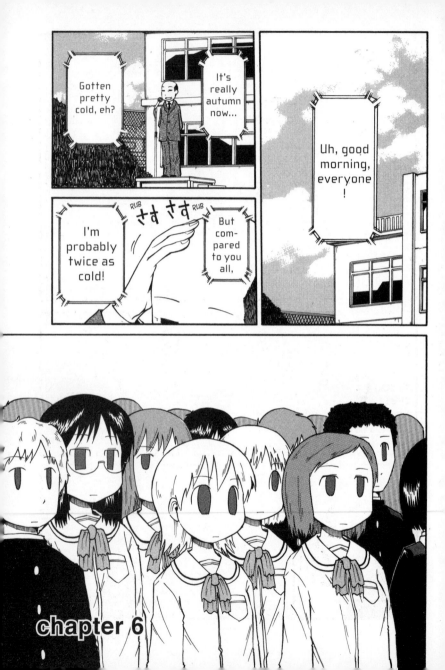

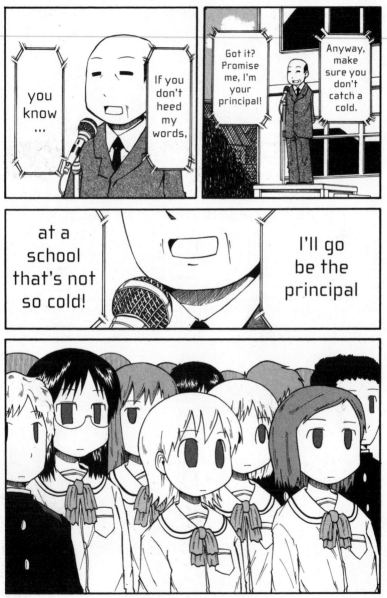

No, no... He must be the most aware of any of us that they always fall flat.

Does the principal not realize that his jokes are way too dated?

And the PTA has...

If that's the case, then our principal is...

highly skilled !!!

in fact,

he keeps going even though he knows we won't laugh, to show us disillusioned youth the persistent spirit of our elders?!

Ah! Unless...

pfft pfft...

M-Mai ?!!

?

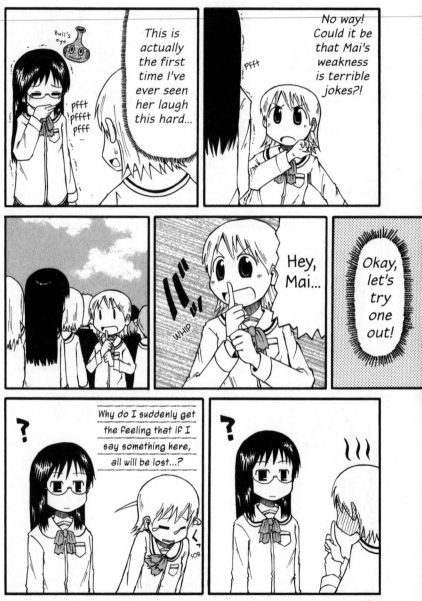

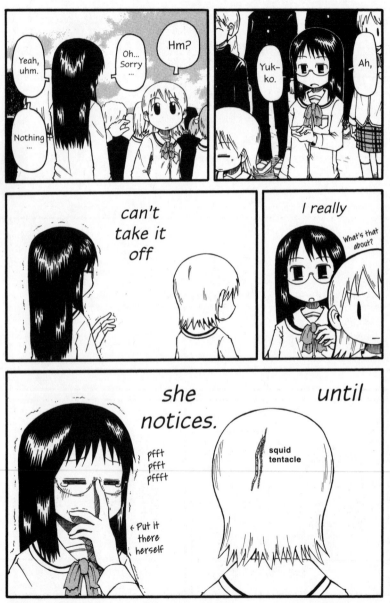

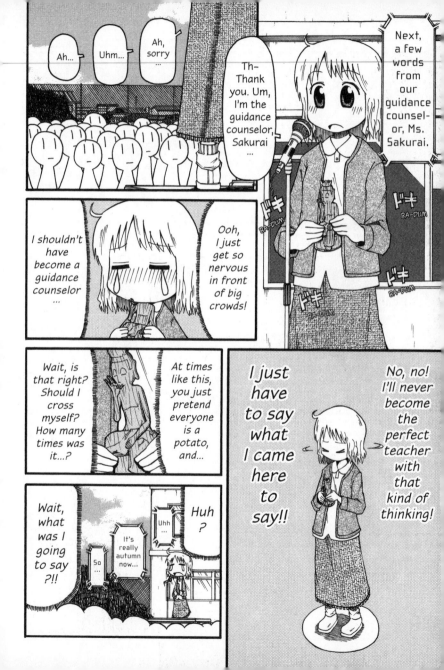

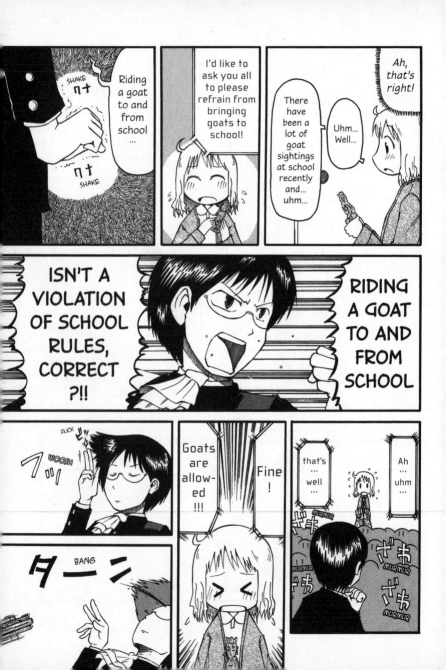

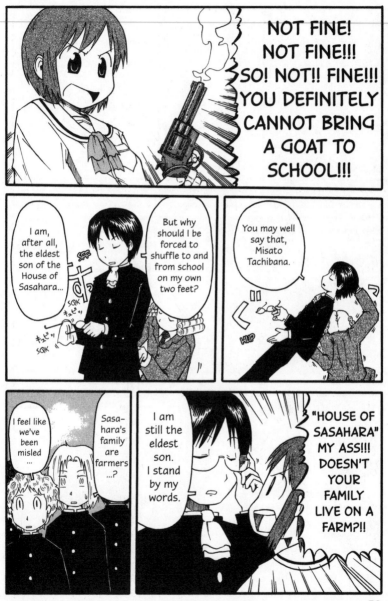

58

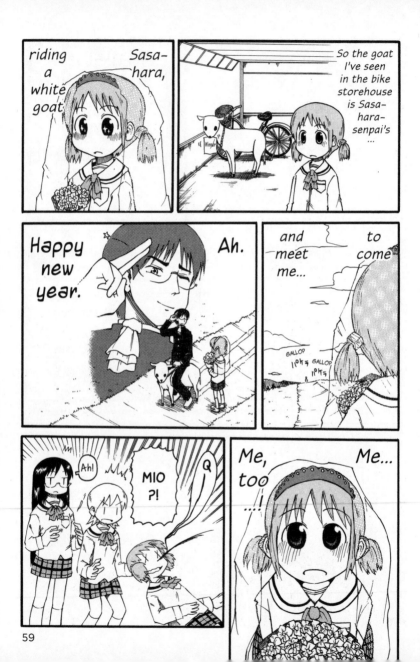

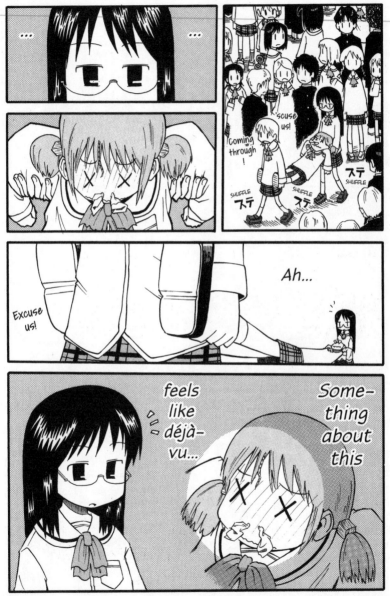

60

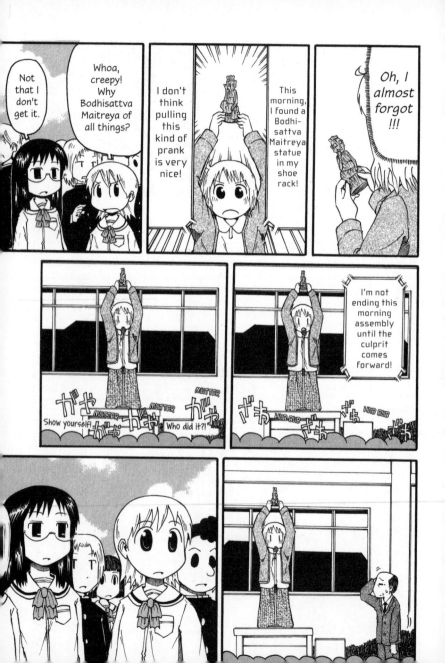

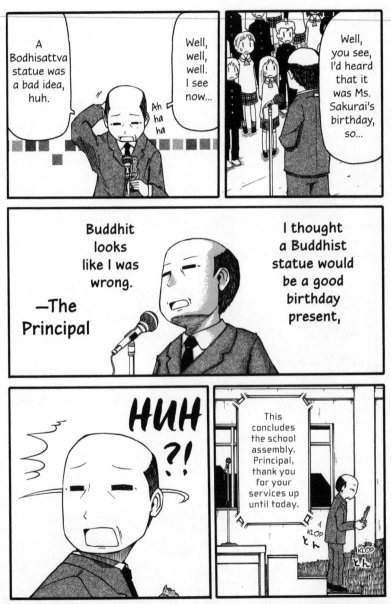

chapter 6: end

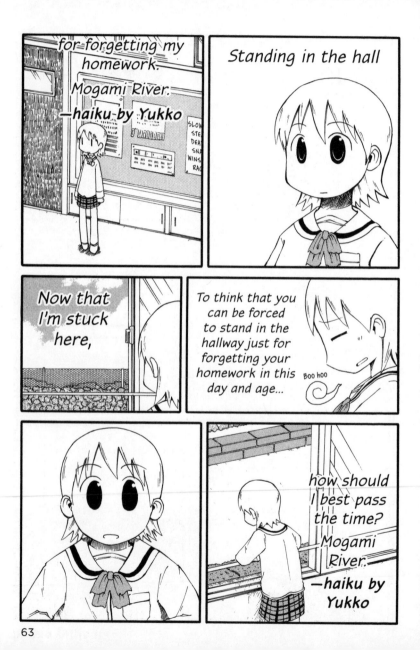

63

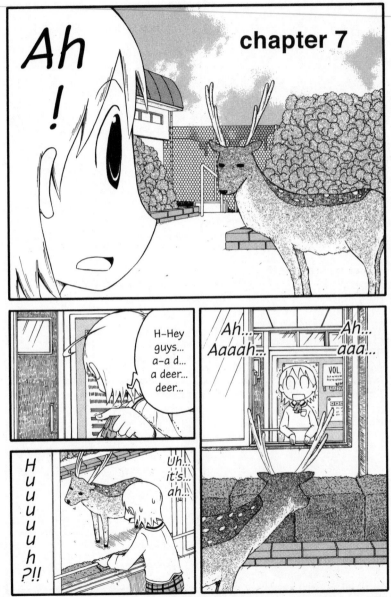

chapter 7

64

Whaaaat?!!
?!!
Hey... guys... the principal... a deer...
ヒョッ WHLIP
ヒョッ WHLIP
Huuuuuh?!!
Uh... it's... ah...
Why is the principal ...
facing down a deer?!!

Whaaaat!!!...

SLAM

Hey... guys...the principal... is dying...

Huuuuuh?!!

Uh... ah... huh?

SFF

Princi- paaal !!!

nngk...

ngk...

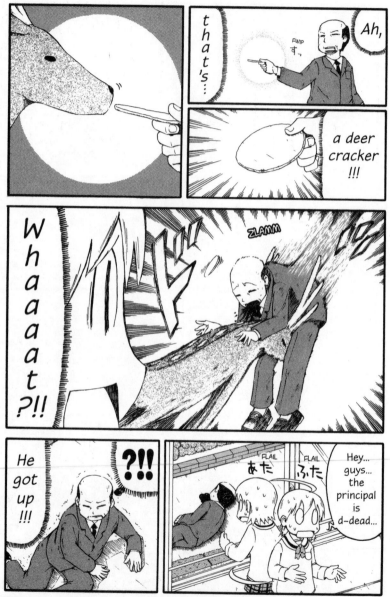

67

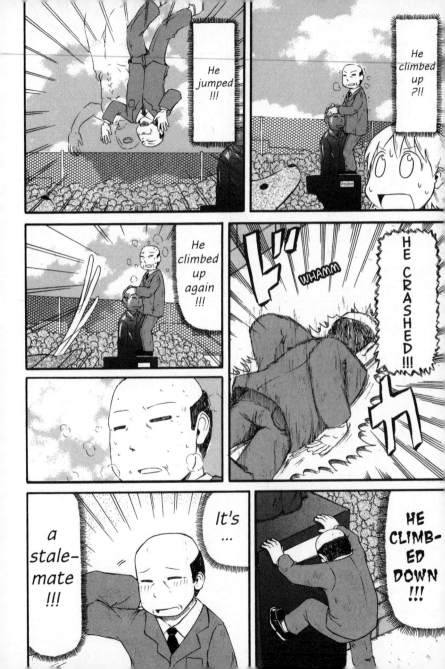

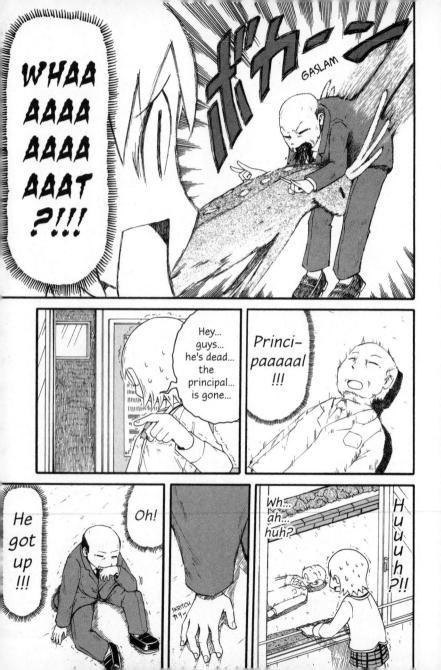

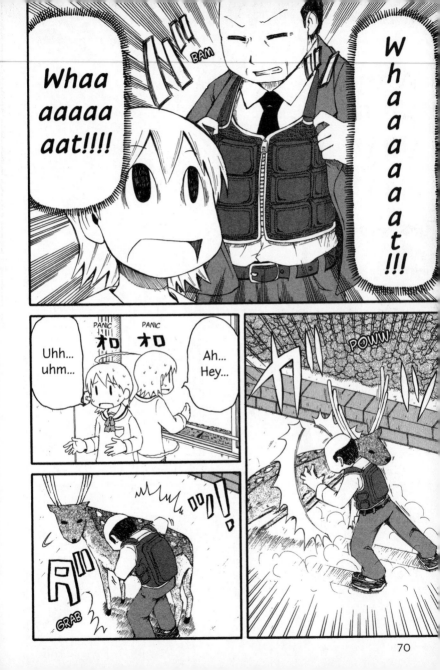

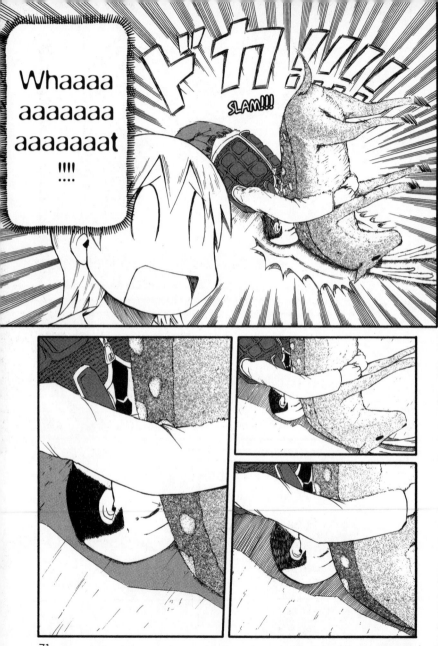

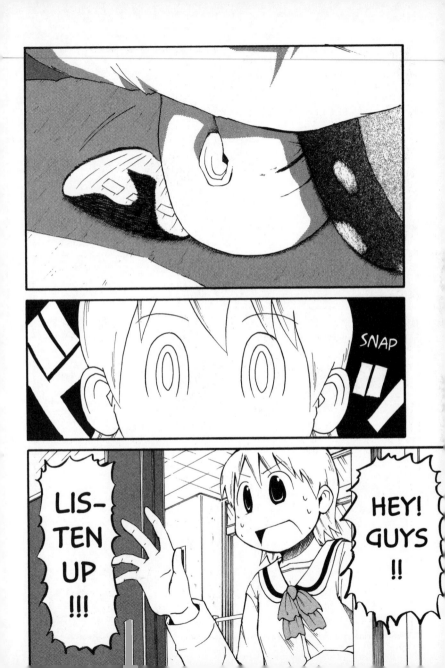

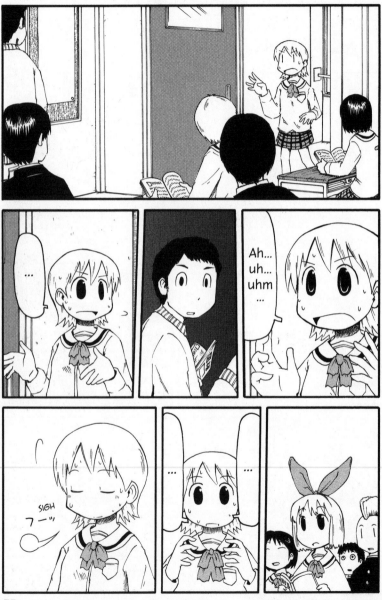

Ah...
uh...
uhm
...

...

SIGH

...   ...

73

WHPP

ALL IS

A-OK OUT IN THE HALL-WAY!!!

It wasn't to protect the principal, or because it would be too hard to explain.

were the truth, spoken from the bottom of my heart.

These words

Heh. I don't get it.

heh heh heh

Gathering the rains of early summer. Swiftly: Mogami River.

Perhaps it was just a way of showing respect to the heroes who had played out their life-or-death struggle before me.

chapter 7: end

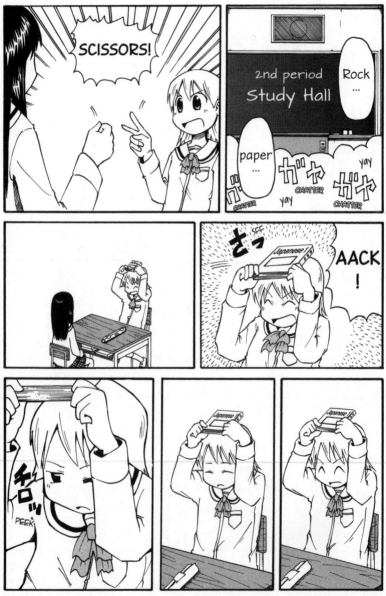

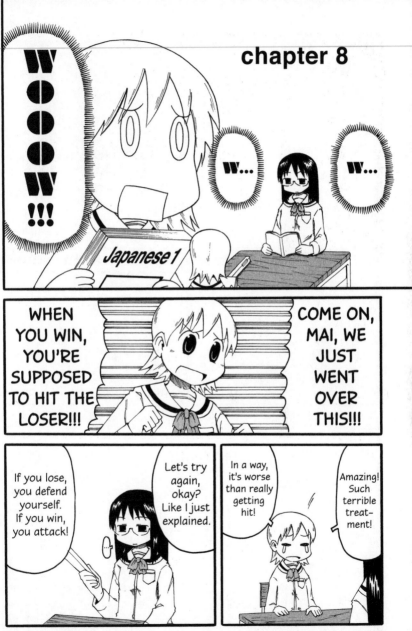

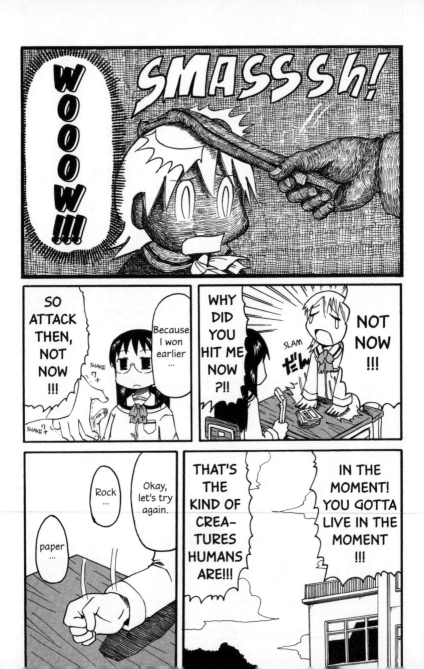

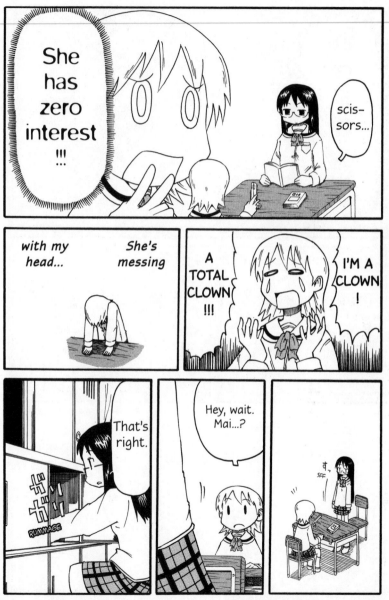

78

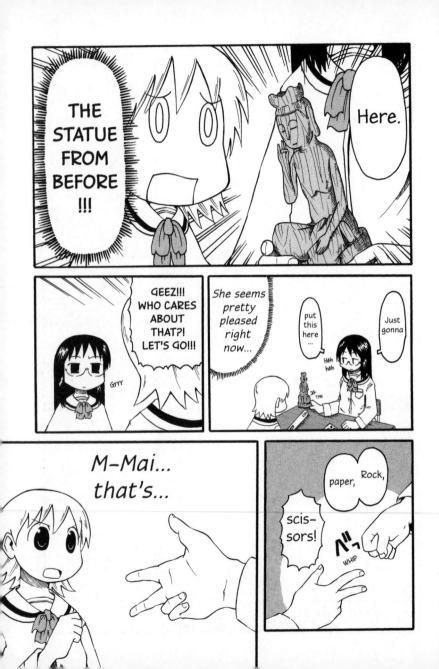

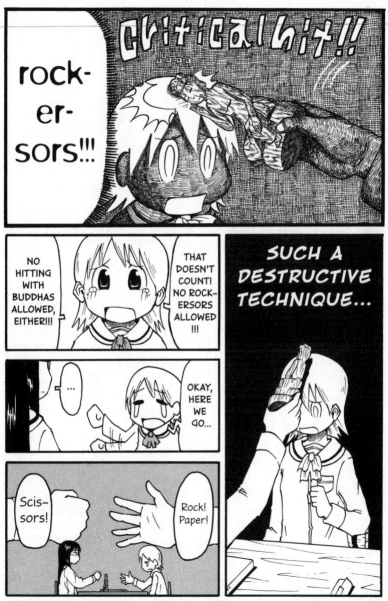

WHAAAAAPPP

SHINNNG

Okay, let's go again!

...

See? You can totally do it!

Yes! That's it!! That's it, Mai!!!

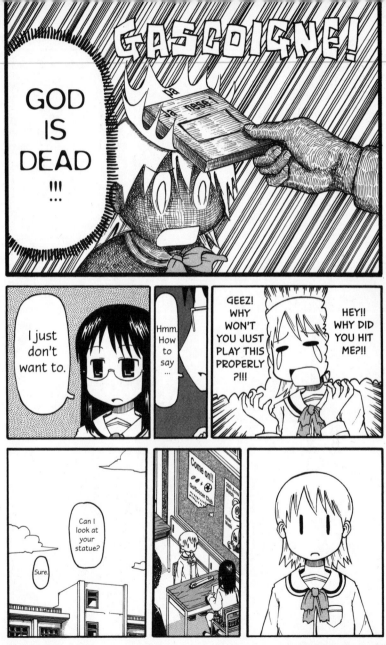

chapter 8: end

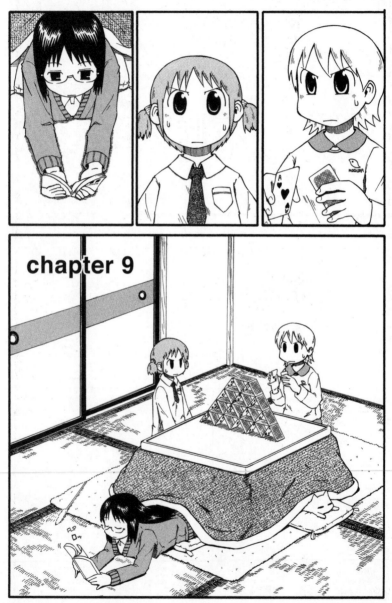

chapter 9

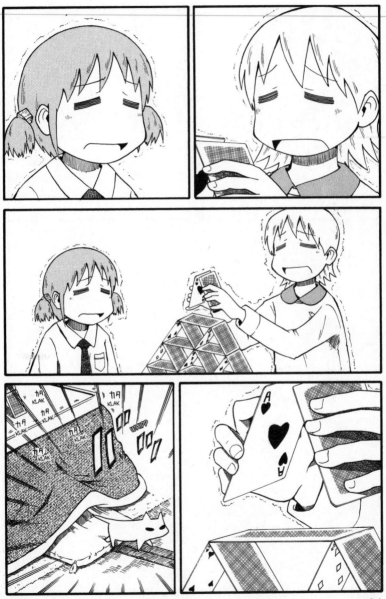

84

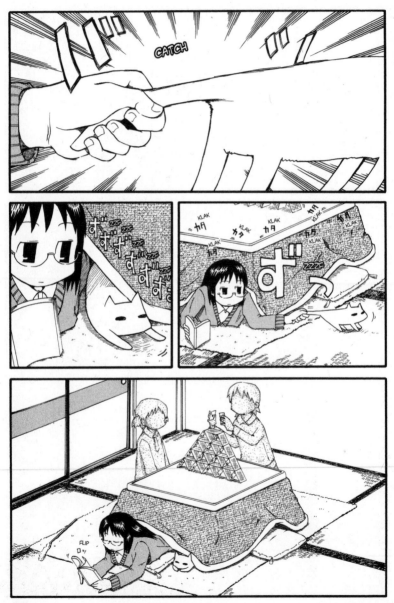

85

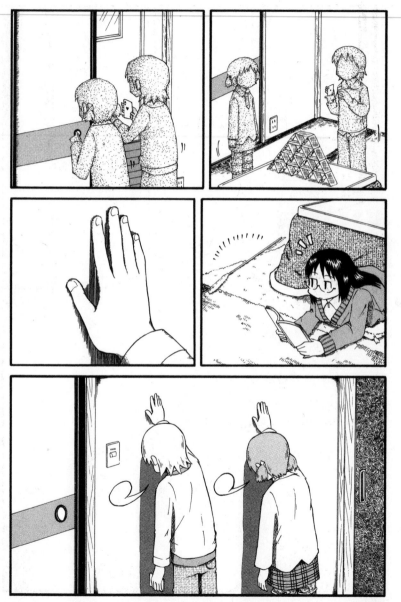

86

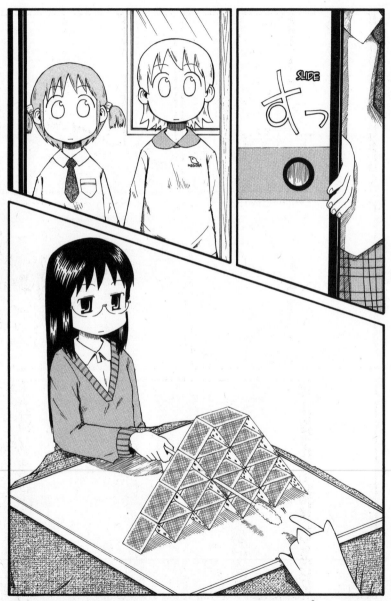

SLIDE
すっ

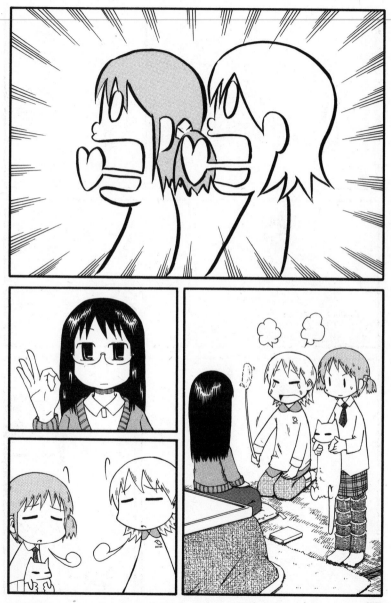

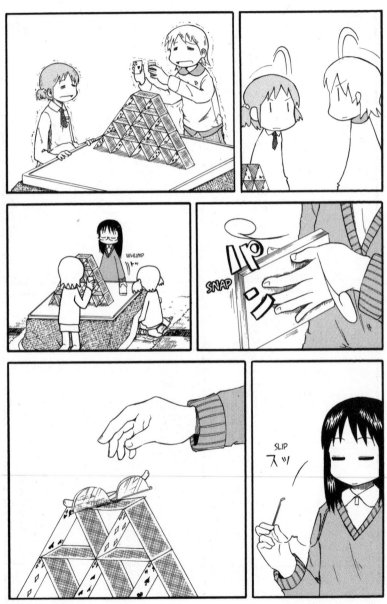

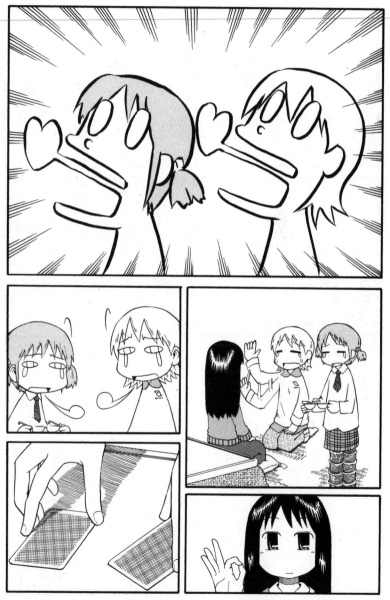

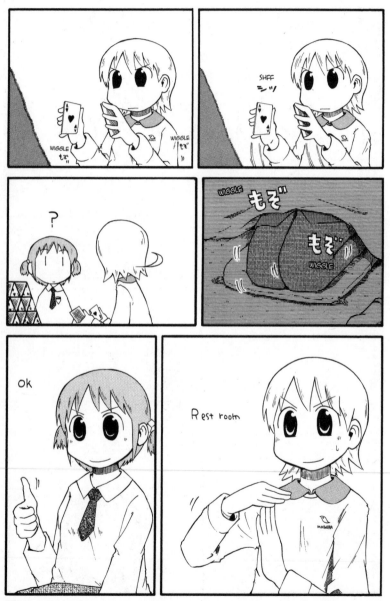

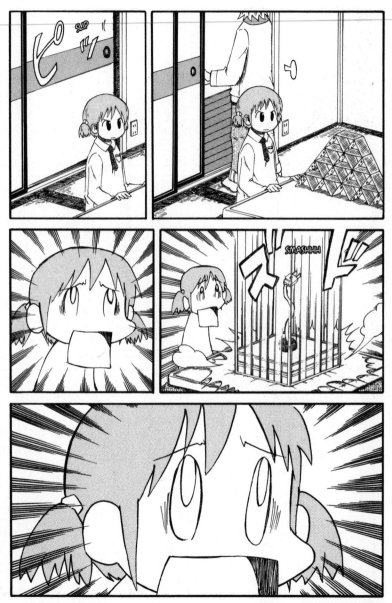

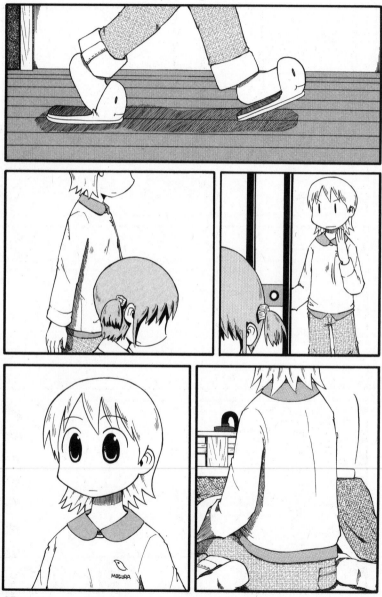

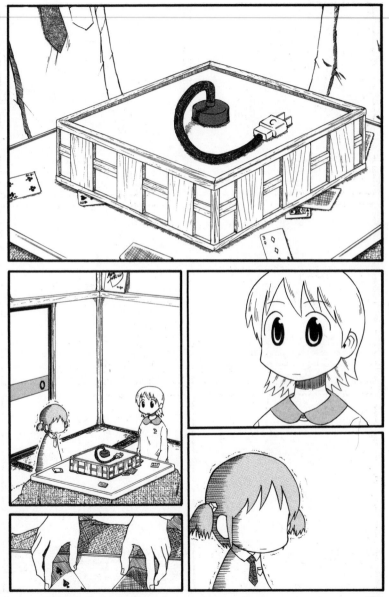

94

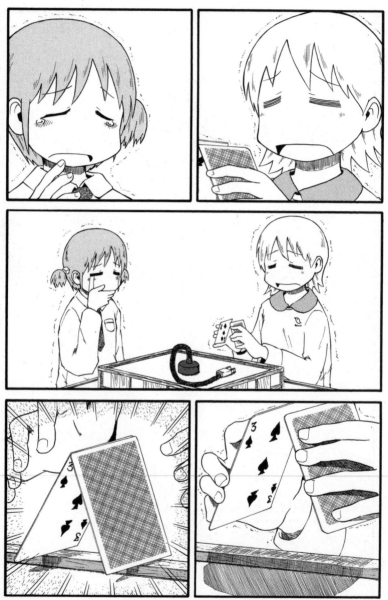

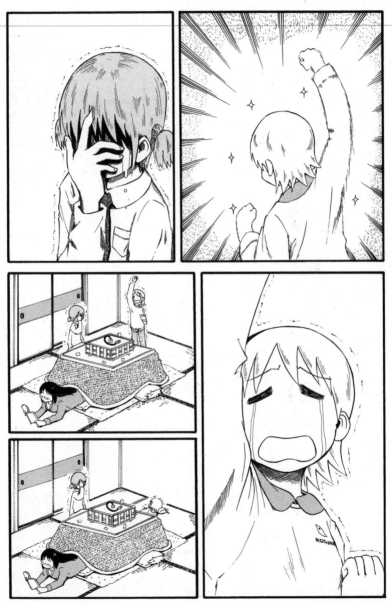

chapter 9: end

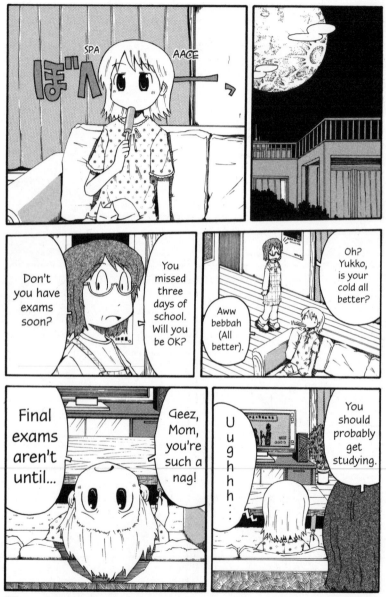

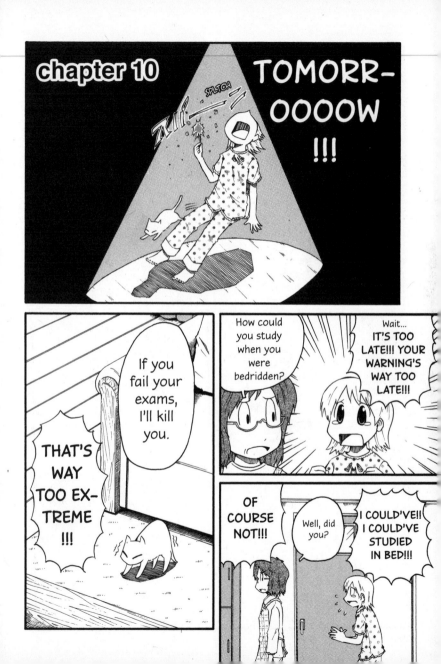

I've got about 10 hours before school starts.

My only option is to study now!!

I'll live not regretting today.
To laugh at tomorrow's my way.
And all the while
I'll put on a smile
And keep my worries at bay.

I can focus just on studying English.

The good news is that tomorrow's tests are English and music.

Final Exam Schedule

	Day 1	Day 2	Day 3
	English	Phys Ed	Japanese
	Music		Math
			Science
			History

and focus.

SWIP

I need to leave behind the depraved failure I was until yesterday

Okay, finished!

by Yukko.

99

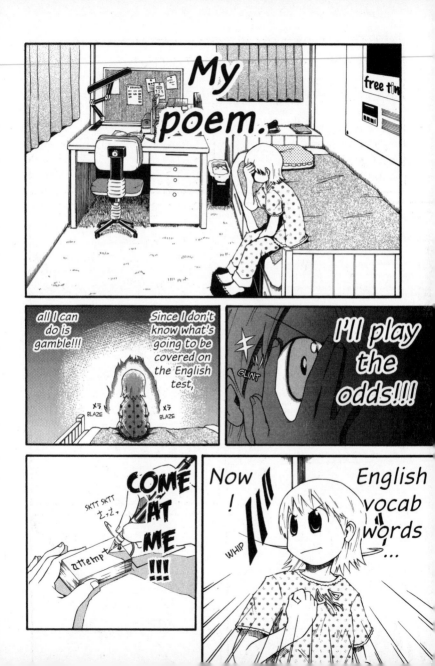

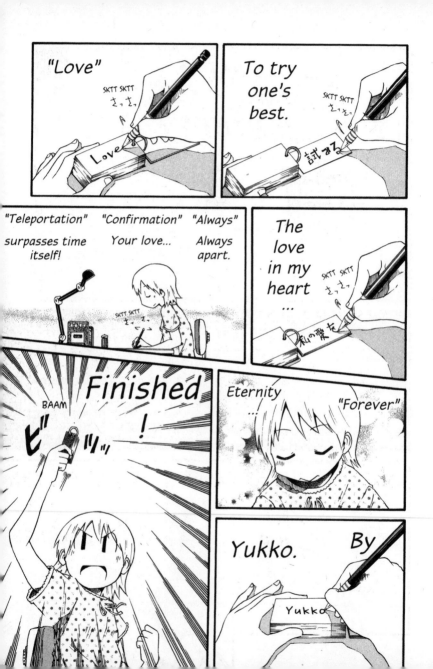

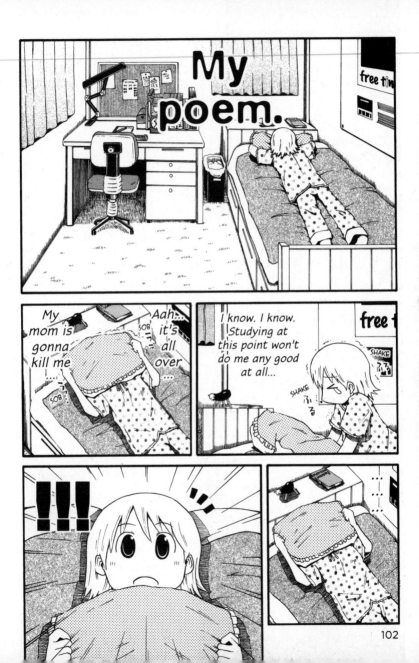

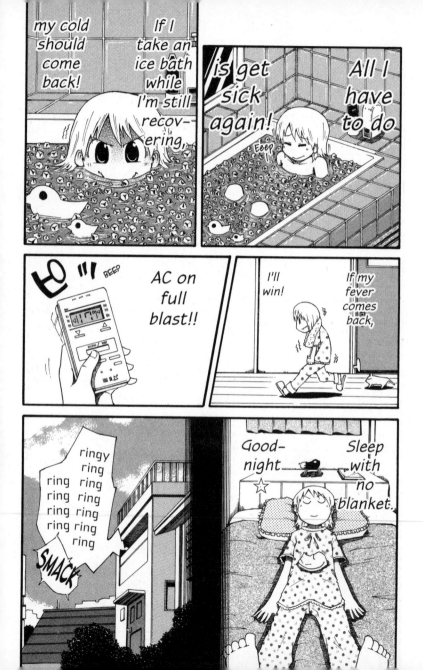

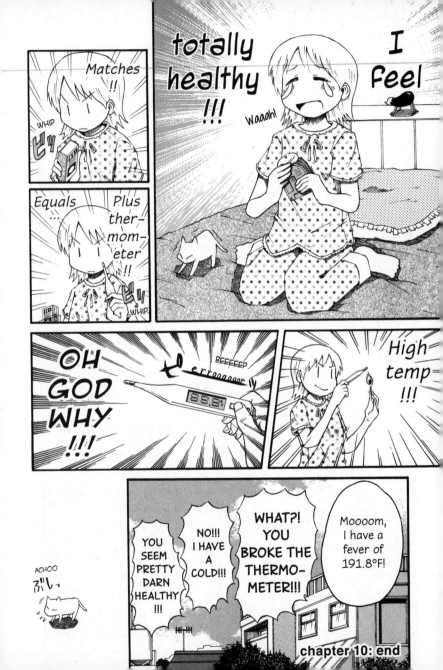

I'm so screwed.

1-Q

Final Exams
English 9:10 ~ 9:55
Phys Ed 10:05 ~ 10:50

I'm totally lost.

Right from the first question

chapter 11

If I panic, I'll screw up the questions I do know!!!

Gotta calm down!! Just calm down, Yukko!!

What English word could possibly fit here ?!!!

First off, what is this thing?!!! It looks like a low-level Dr*gon Quest enemy!!!

jlish Fin

Write the vocabulary, wo

A. (

Write the given Japanese

(2) いつも

(3) スピーチ

(4) 休明

106

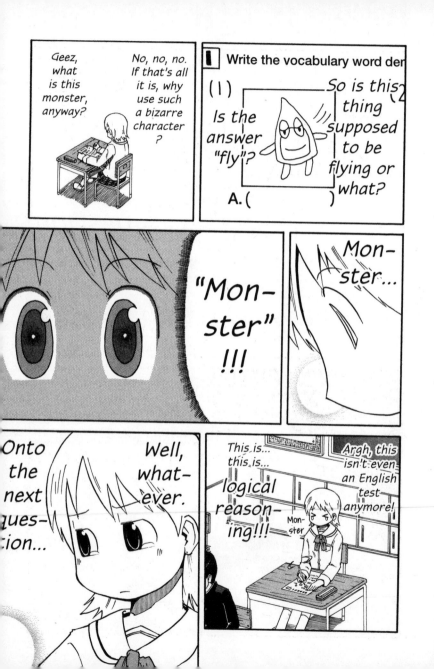

AAAAGH

ish Final Exam

in the picture.

(2)

A.(   )

word in English.

(2) いつも

Anyways, gotta get my eraser.

Which can only mean that "monster" wasn't the answer to the last one!! What's up with these trick questions?!!

It's the monster again, with a tennis racket ...

POP

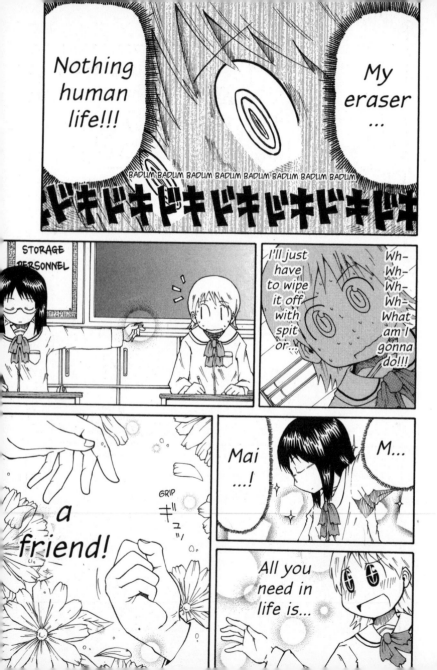

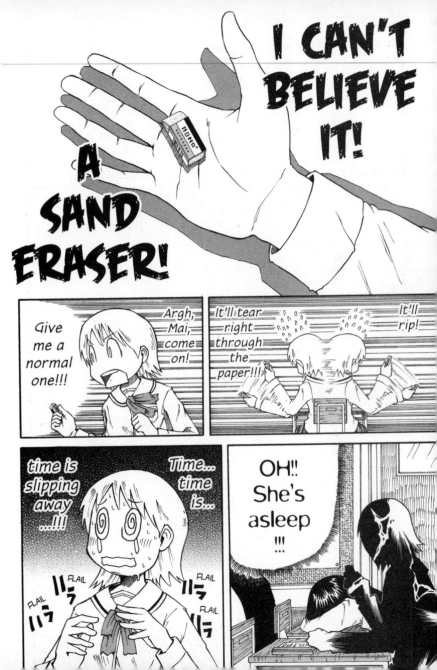

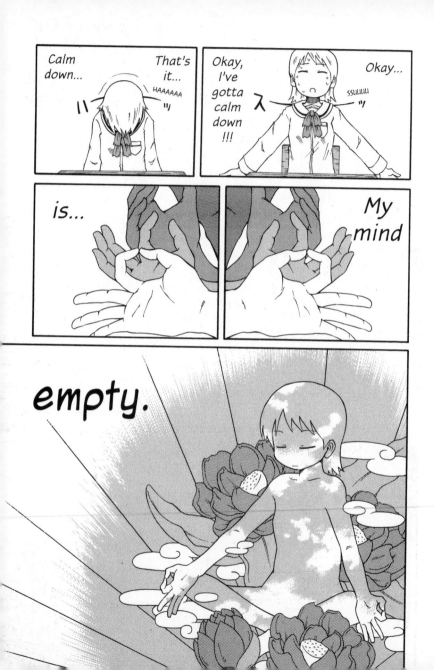

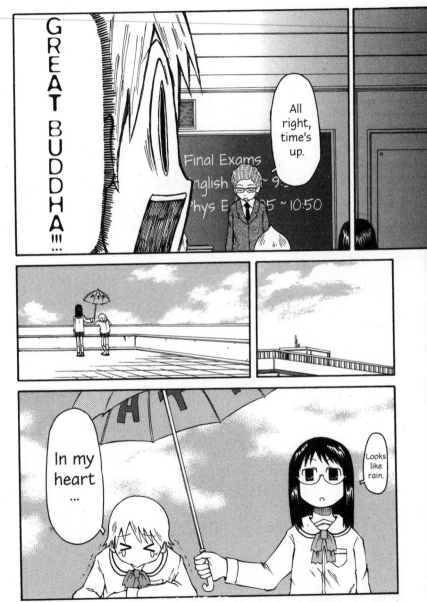

chapter 11: end

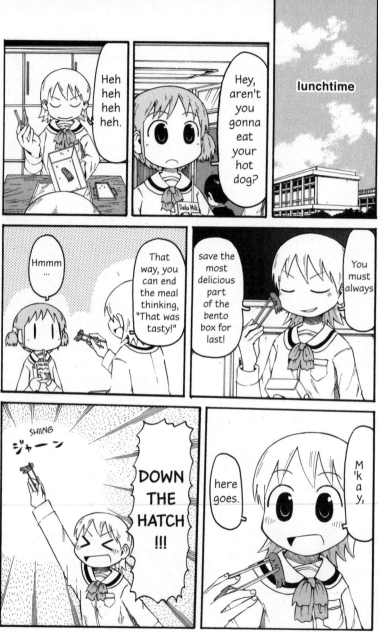

113

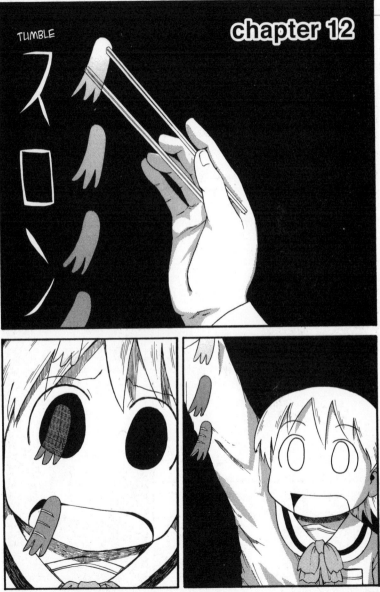

TUMBLE

chapter 12

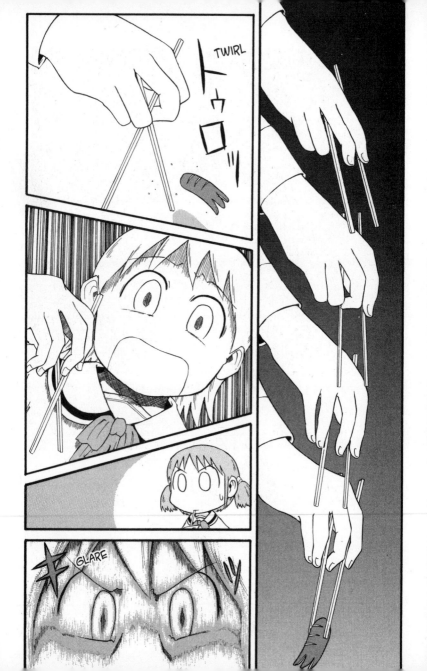

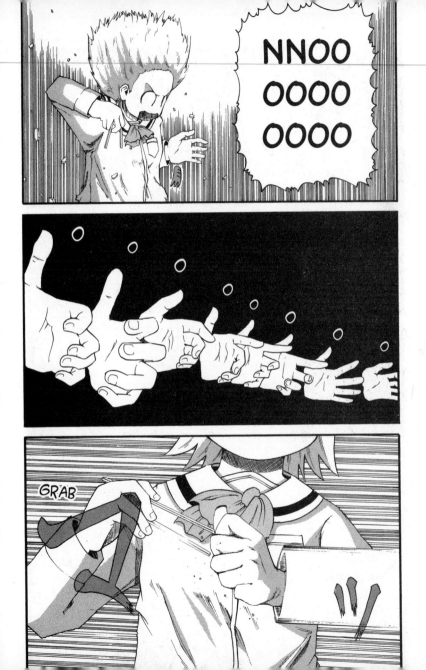

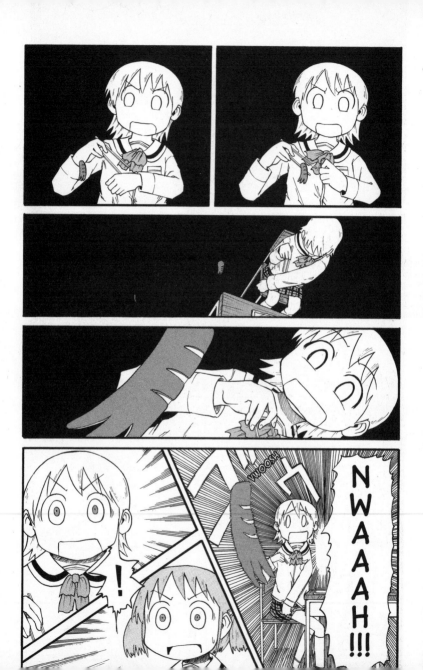

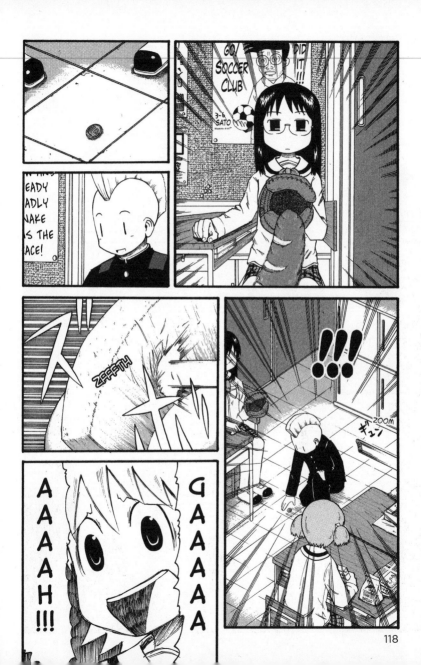

118

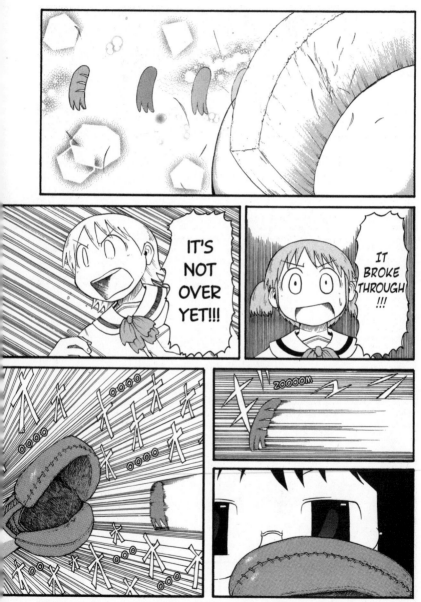

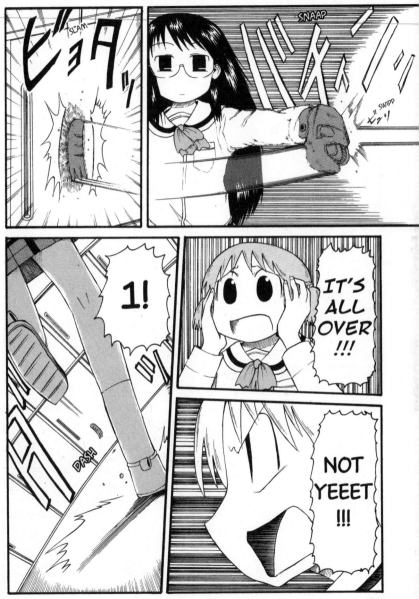

120

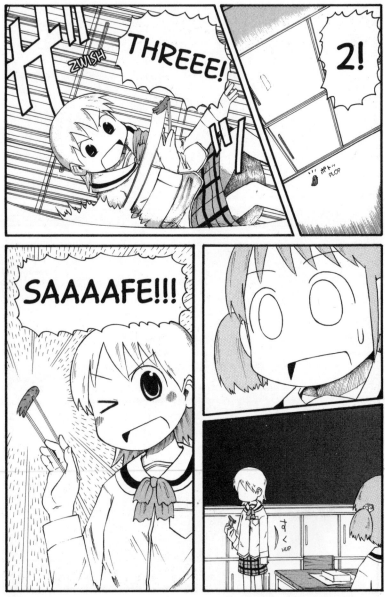

121

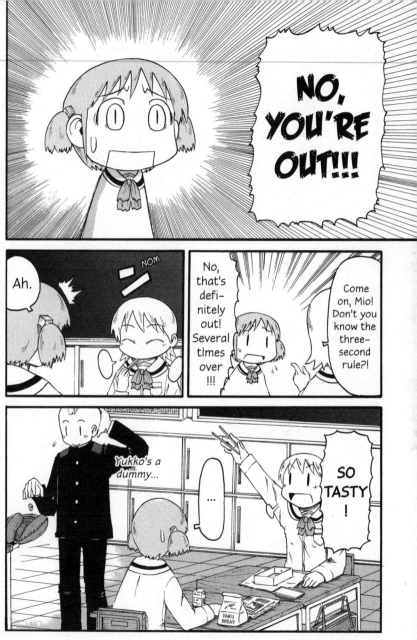

chapter 12: end

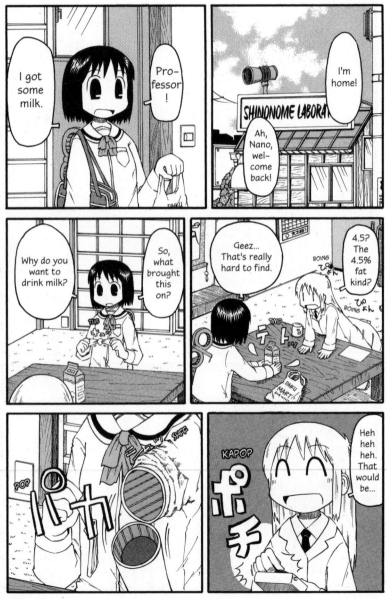

chapter 13

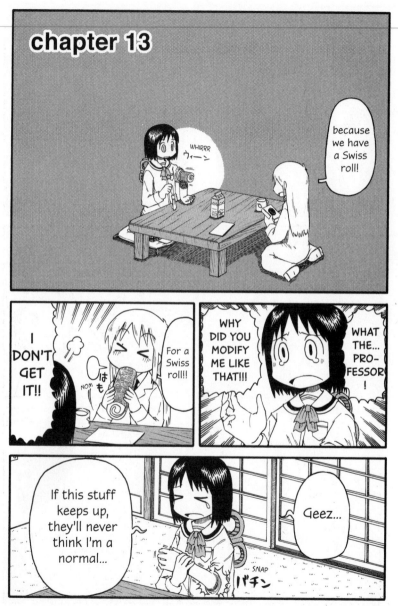

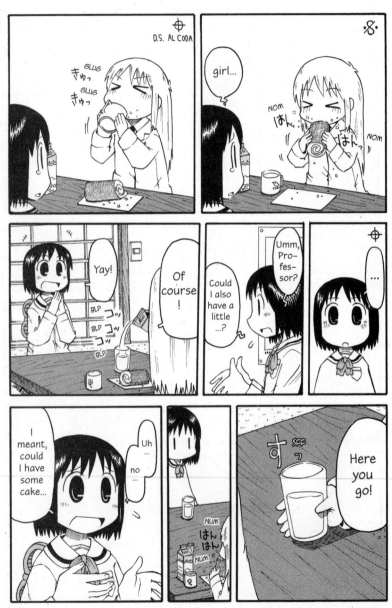

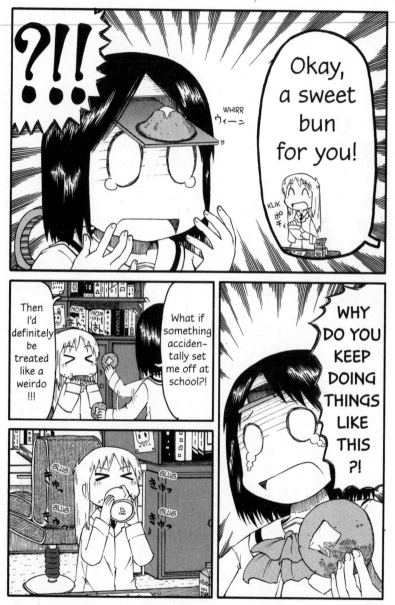

126

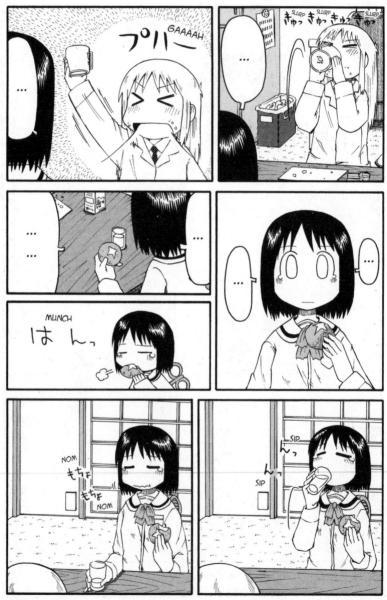

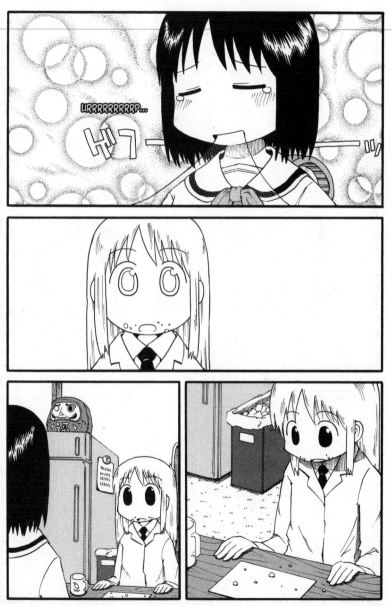

128

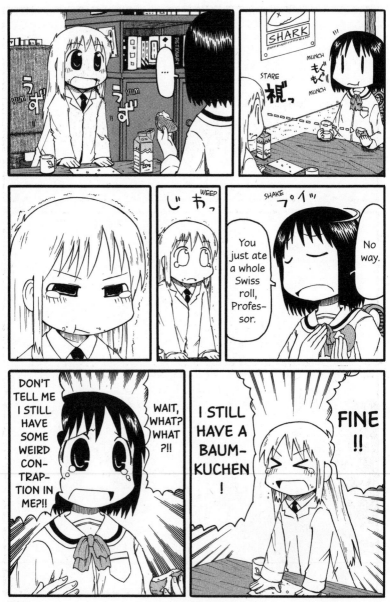

129

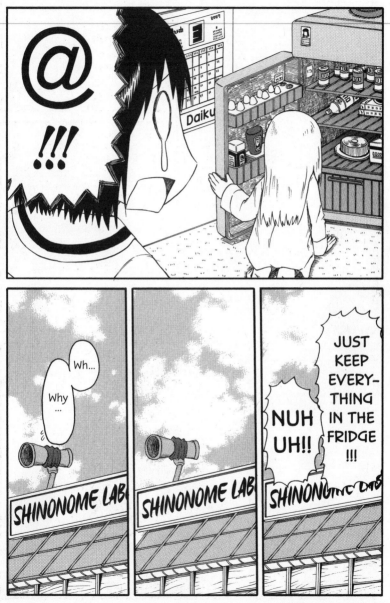

chapter 13: end

Recently there's been a decline in morality in the school...

So,

Principal Office

what- ever I do...

I–I'll do...

I'd like to ask you, as the guidance counselor, to be more strict with the students.

Y–Yes sir!

Gotta stop being so timid and take charge!!

That's right! I became the guidance counselor to improve myself.

chapter 14

COCONUT MILK

JOLT

ビクッ

131

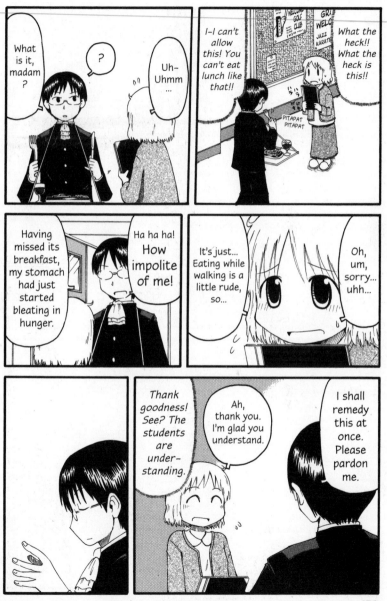

132

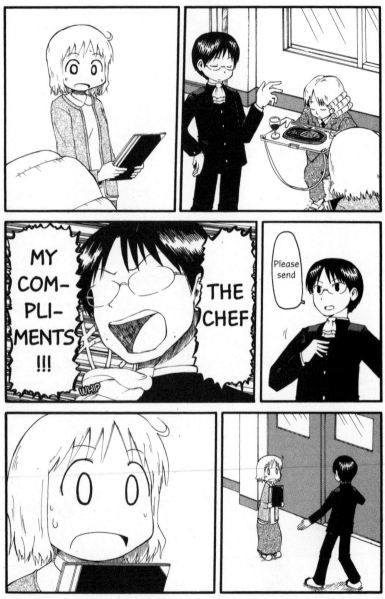

MY COMPLIMENTS!!!

THE CHEF

Please send

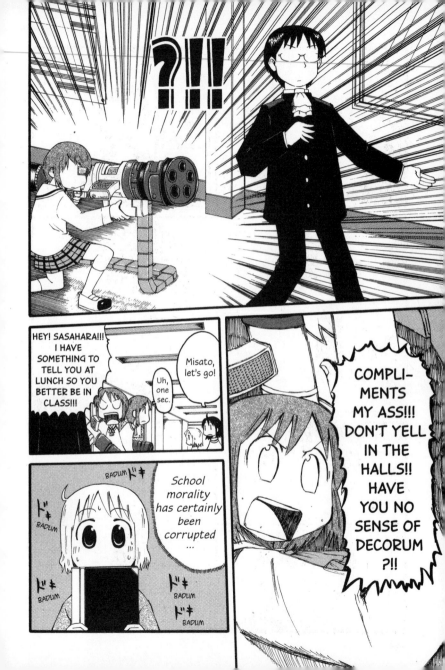

Ah, this old thing?

Hmm?

What's the frilly thing around your neck?

Oh, right.

It's cute...!

Ah, sure... No problem...

Apologies. Misato Tachibana meant no ill will by that. Please pardon her.

Ordinarily extraordinary days, as it were.

might perhaps be a succession of miracles.

The ordinary lives that all of us lead every day

SHOCK

PFFFT

what is that frilly thing...?

So then... Ah.

135

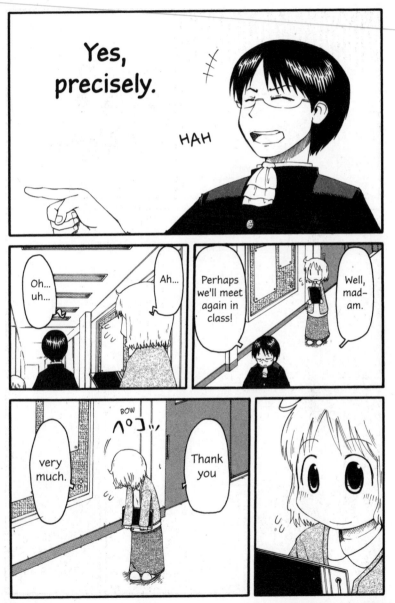

chapter 14: end

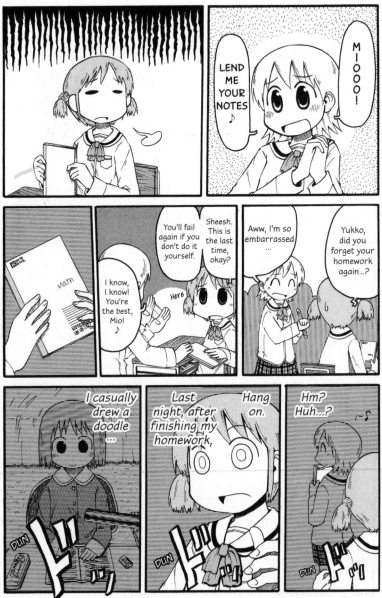

137

chapter 15

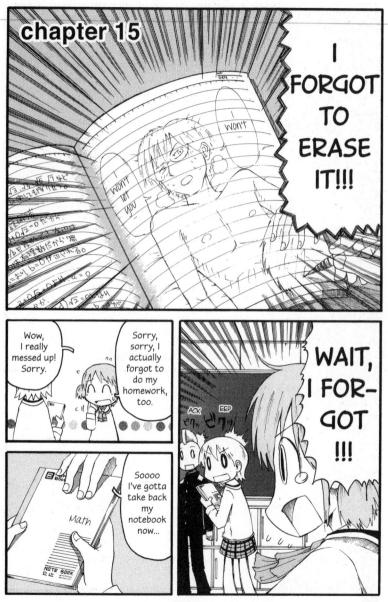

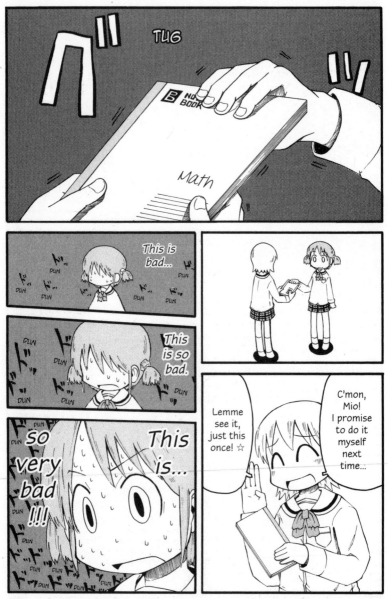

And if the one to see it is Yukko, of all people...

If anyone sees that I drew that kind of thing, they'll never look at me the same way again.

AT THE SPEED OF SOUND!!!

FLASH

Rumors will spread

But this one says "Math"...

?

My math notebook is this one here.

Ha ha

Ah, silly me... That's my Japanese notebook.

6 Diary

140

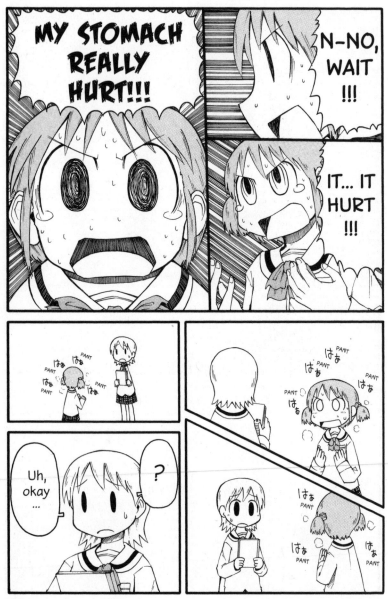

...This is it...

Anyways, I'll make copies right away, so just hang on a bit.

Yukko!!! That notebook...

ends right here!!!

CLENCH

My high school life...

If she sees that picture...

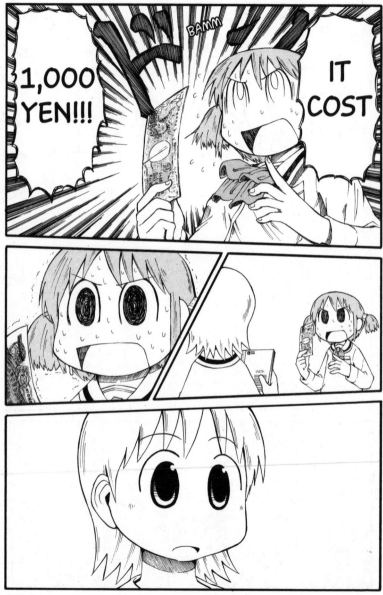

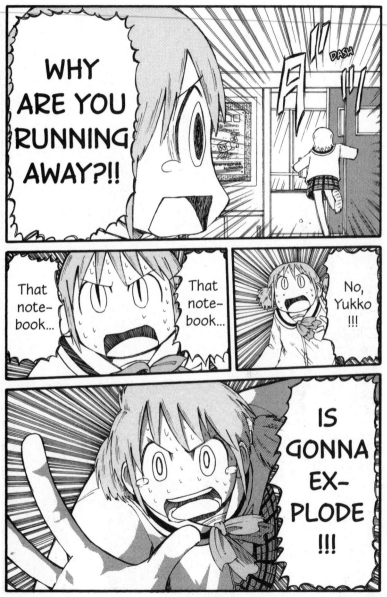

144

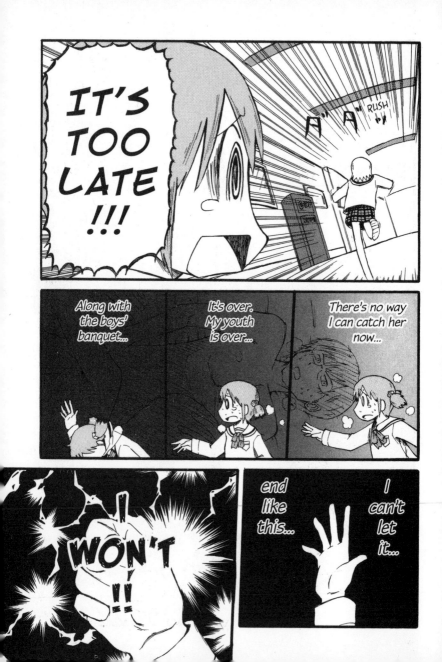

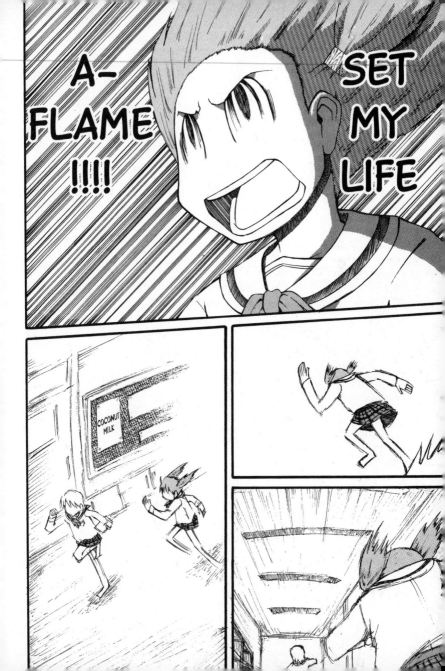

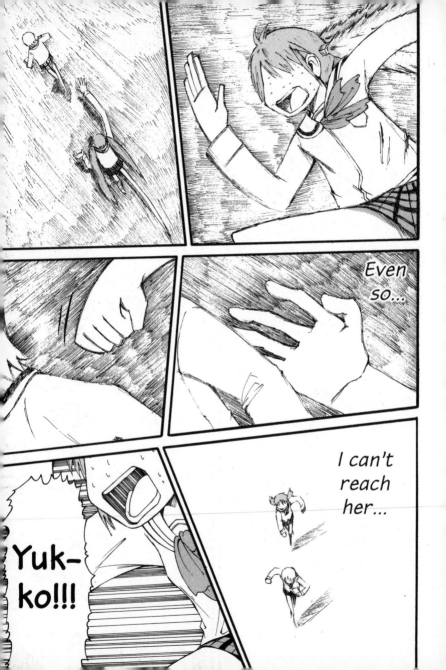

Even so...

I can't reach her...

Yuk-
ko!!!

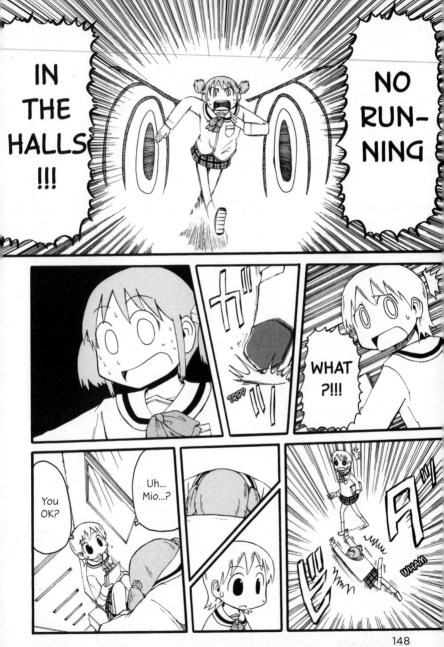

ZOOOOM

SNATCH

...   ...

If you forgot to do your homework, please speak up!

Spend our youth working towards our dreams together.
– Class 1-2

Please pass your notebooks forward!

CHATTER   CHATTER

Here

Thanks.

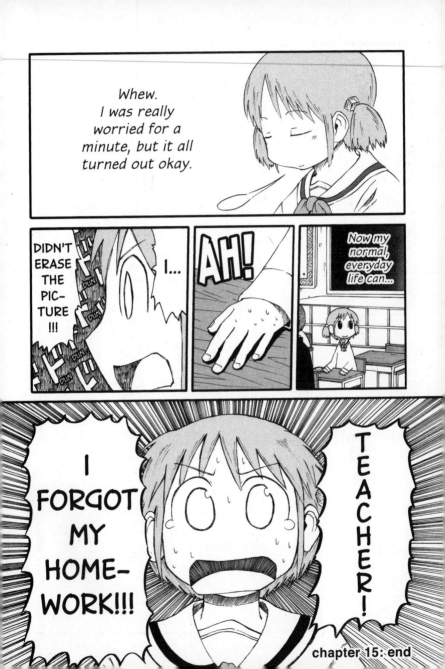

chapter 15: end

sunday

CHIRP

CHIRP

COCKA-DOODLE-DOO

?

What's up, sis?

Good timing.

Oh, Mio.

YAAWN

Besides, they'll pay 10,000 yen for a day's work.

Mom's at a kick volleyball match with her friends.

What? Why? Get mom to do that kind of thing!

Can you help me with the neighborhood association event?

Listen, something just came up...

FWIP

NEIGHBORHOOD ASSOCIATION
DAIFUKU FAIR
DAIFUKU!!
DAIFUKU

Well, since I have nothing better to do...

10,000 yen in a day sure is nice...

chapter 16

How did I get into this mess ...?

This is the worst! What is this? What the hell is this?

I've been had !!!

I...

This is...

DAIFUKU FAIR

They're white!

DAIFUKU FAIR

Daifuku

Daifuku Fair

And this "neighborhood association event" is just me and this guy selling daifuku on the street!

MR. DAIFUKU

152

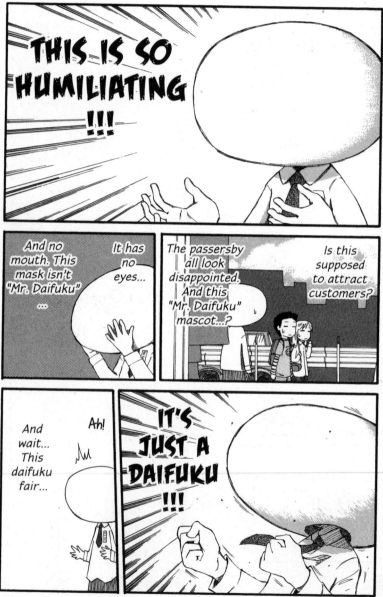

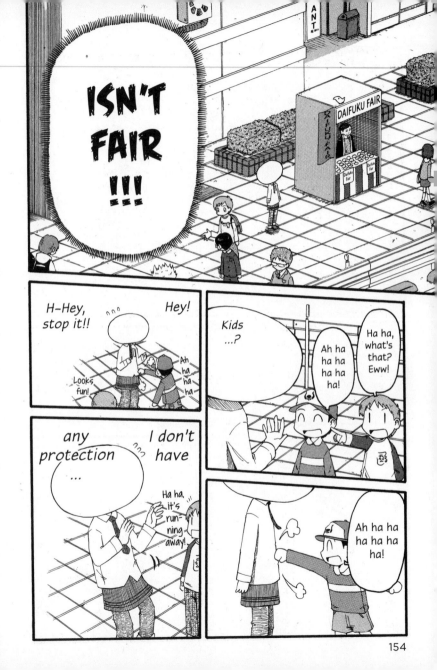

My body
is totally unpro-tected!!!
Ah ha ha ha
Kill it!!
ENOO-OOUGH!!
KNOCK IT OFF!!!
Wah!!! It's mad!!!
Run away!!
Yeaah!
Argh, geez, kids these days...
Whew
THUP THUP
だだっ
Ah ha ha
?

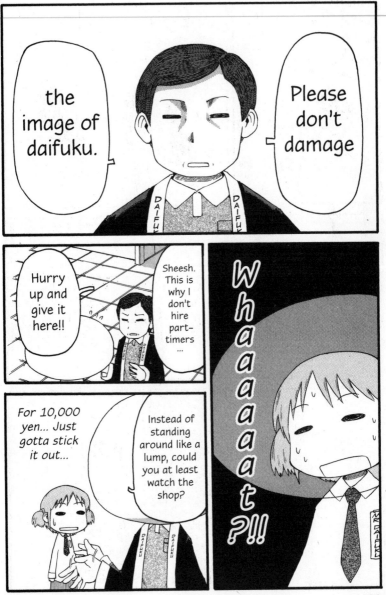

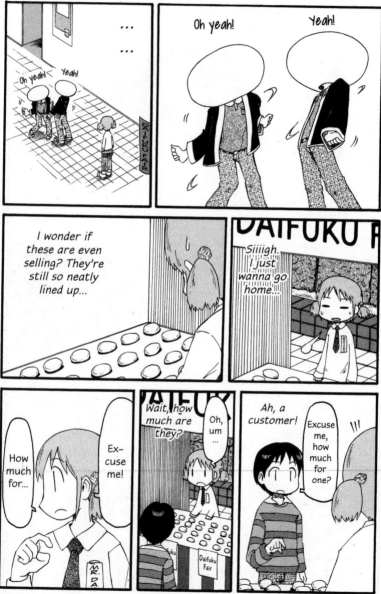

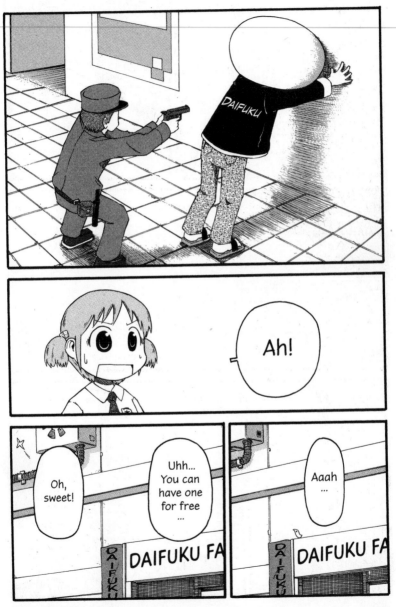

chapter 16: end

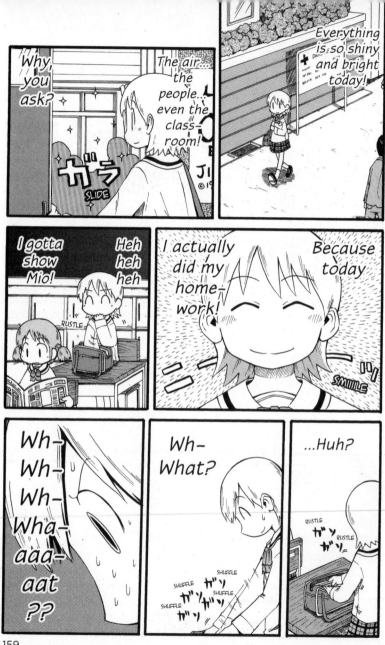

159

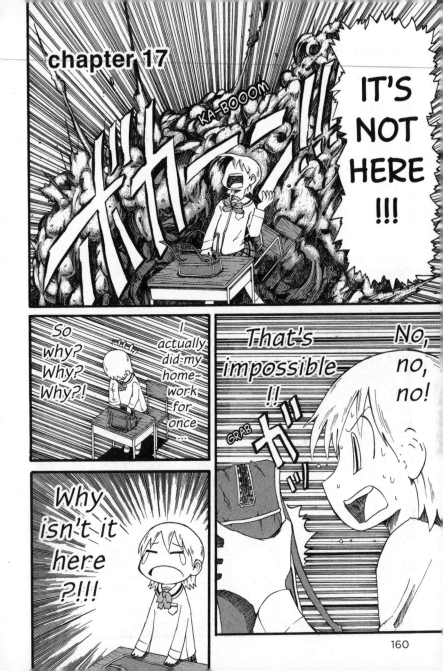

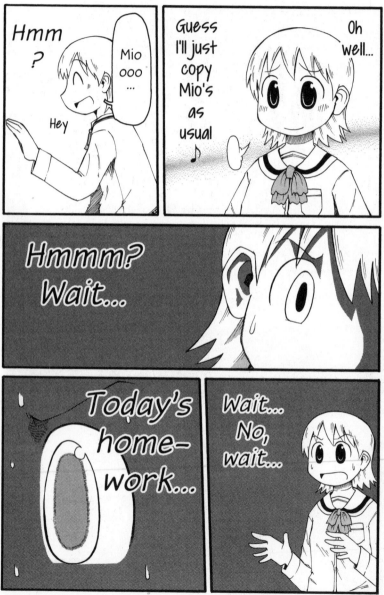

161

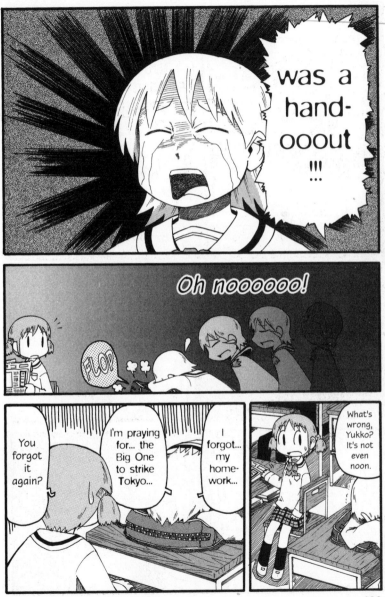

162

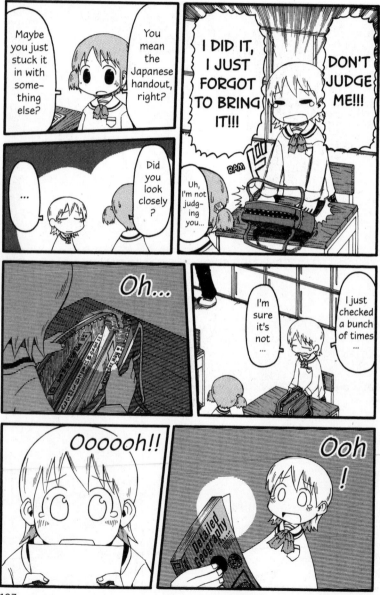

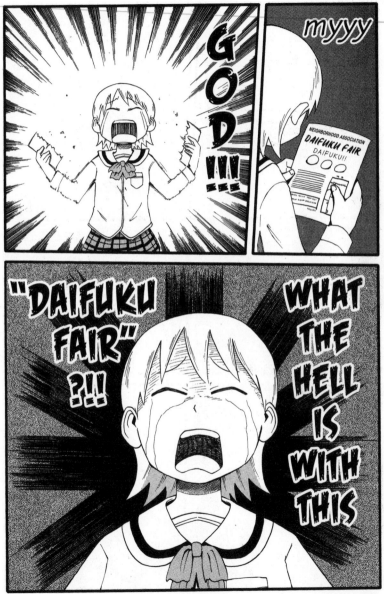

164

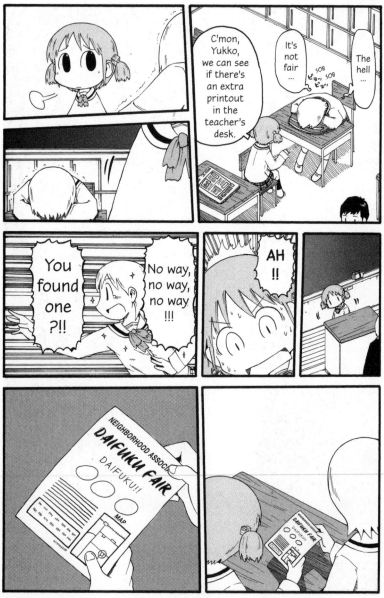

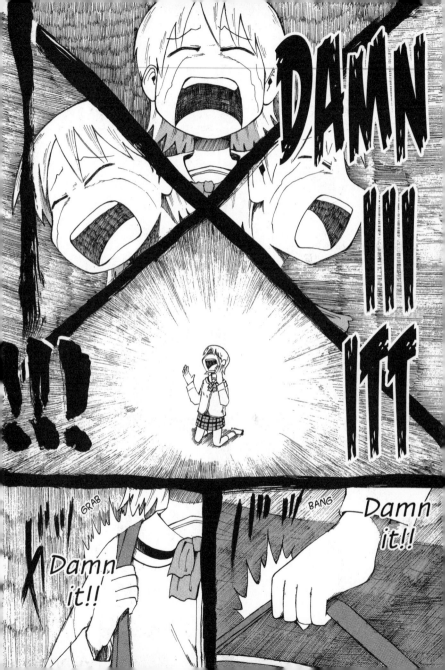

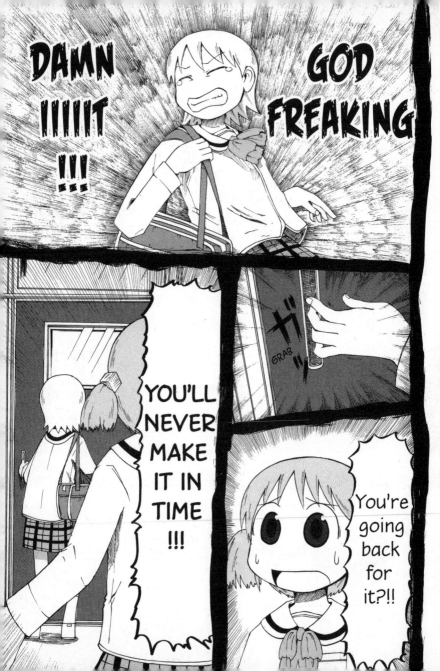

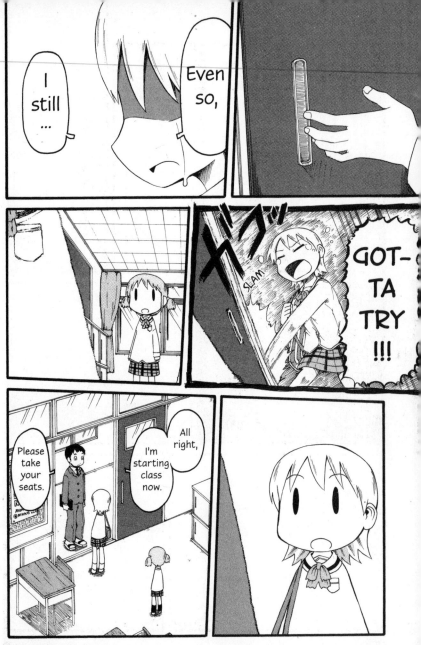

chapter 17: end

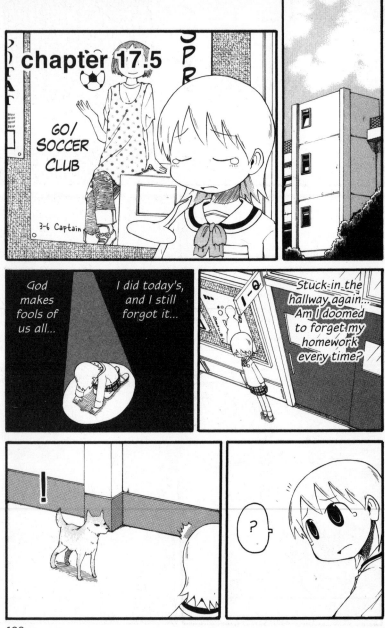

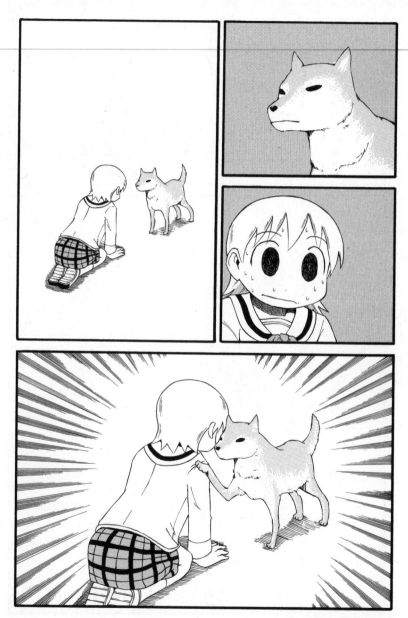

chapter 17.5: end

It's really a nuisance at school!

Would you please take this wind-up key off my back already?

Pro-fes-sor!

Pro-fes-sor!

Ah, Nano, wel-come back!

SHINONOME L

That?

...

And when we played soccer, I kept getting called offside...

Like today, in gym,

I could only do a belly roll!

WHUNK

I can take it.

chapter 18

171

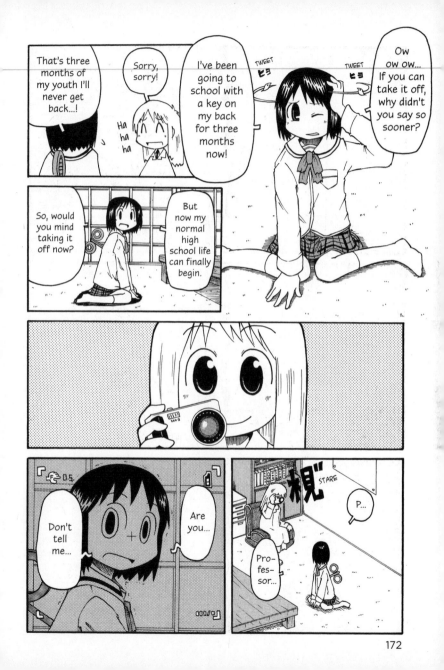

172

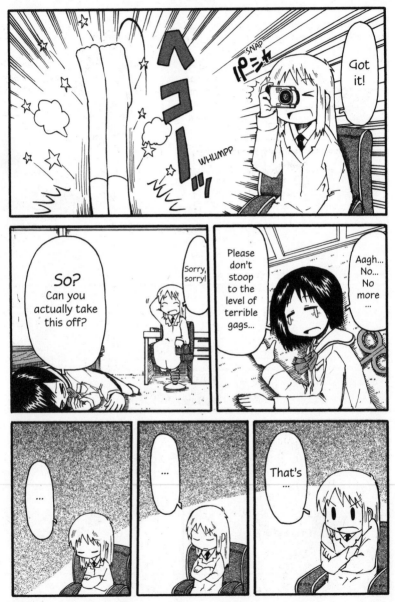

173

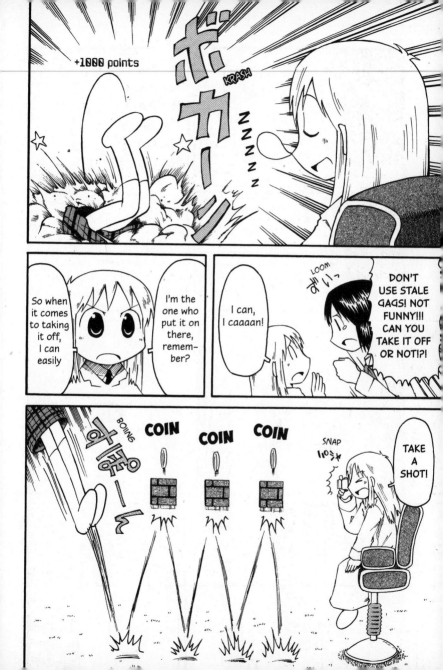

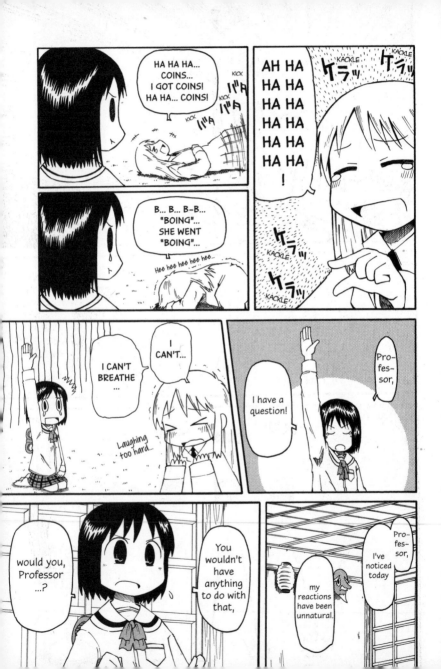

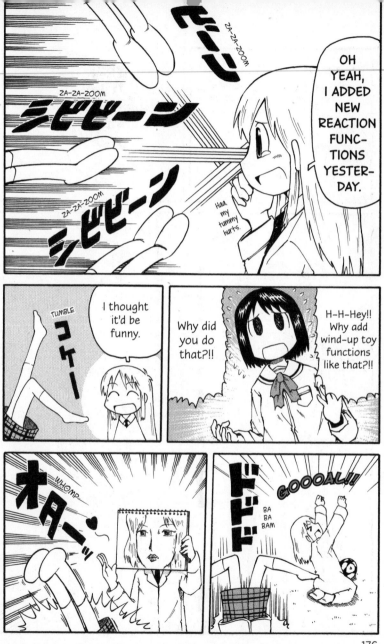

IT'S NOT FUNNY!!!

Pretty funny, though, right?

Waaaaah

I'm gonna die from over-reactions...

I'm gonna die...

get rid of this function!

CHINONOME LABORAT

For now, could you please...

We can worry about the key later, so...

CHEAP-SKATE!

Okay, that'll be 100 yen ♡

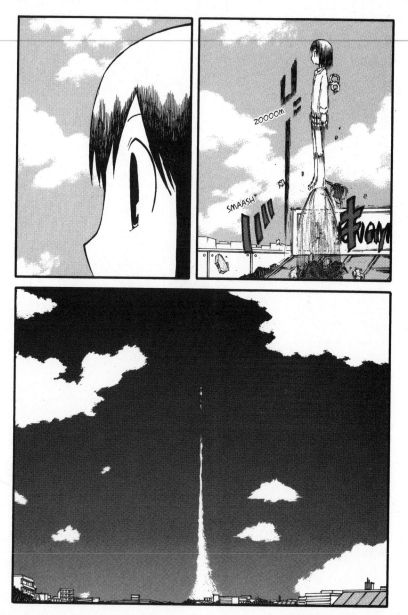

chapter 18: end

to be continued in volume 2~♪

nichijou 1

my ordinary life

A Vertical Comics Edition

Translation: Jenny McKeon
Production: Grace Lu
           Hiroko Mizuno

© Keiichi ARAWI 2007
Edited by KADOKAWA SHOTEN
First published in Japan in 2007 by KADOKAWA CORPORATION, Tokyo.
English translation rights arranged with KADOKAWA CORPORATION, Tokyo
through TUTTLE-MORI AGENCY, INC., Tokyo.

Published by Vertical Comics, an imprint of Vertical, Inc., New York

Originally published in Japanese as *nichijou 1* by Kadokawa Corporation, 2007
nichijou first serialized in *Monthly Shonen Ace,* Kadokawa Corporation, 2006-2015

This is a work of fiction.

ISBN: 978-1-942993-30-8

Manufactured in Canada

First Edition

Second Printing

Vertical, Inc.
451 Park Avenue South
7th Floor
New York, NY 10016
www.vertical-comics.com

Vertical books are distributed through Penguin-Random House Publisher Services.